For Business Ow
Of Chasing

CW00499575

Unlock The Sales Game

New Trust-Based Selling Strategies To Finally
Create Your Sales Breakthrough

ARI GALPER

The World's #1 Authority on Trust-Based Selling
CEO of Unlock The Game®

Published by Unlock The Game
125 Oxford Street, Suite 223
Bondi Junction, NSW 2022 Australia

Email: askus@unlockthegame.com
Website: www.UnlockTheGame.com

Acknowledgements

To my amazing wife Michelle and gorgeous kids Toby, Nathan and Jaime. Thank you so much for all of your loving support over the years in my quest to change the world through trust. To my incredible Unlock The Game team and the work that you do for our private clients, it's magical what you have done and continue to do. Lastly, to my over 70,000 members and clients worldwide, thank you for believing that you can become successful without having to sacrifice your integrity along the way.

Contents

Introduction

If you flick through the pages of business magazines and traditional sales training material, you will find a constant flow of messages like, 'Focus on closing the sale', 'Overcome objections', 'Be relentless', 'Accept rejection as a normal part of selling', 'Use persuasion to get useful information about your prospects' and 'Chase the sale'.

In most cases, it becomes about getting the sale at the expense of the human relationship. For the customer, this approach is transparent and all too familiar. Crossing social boundaries and adding pressure to the sales process makes it a gut-wrenching and painful process for both the seller and the buyer.

In this new economy, there is a much better way to succeed in selling. But it's not for everyone. You'll need to be open minded because it may contradict everything you've been taught about what selling is about.

It begins with moving away from the hidden agenda of focusing on making the sale. When you do this, a new world opens up for you. In other words, when you stop selling and start building authentic relationships based on trust, authenticity and integrity, the possibilities become endless. It's a whole new mindset in selling, which I call Unlock The Game®.

The vast majority of traditional sales techniques contradict everything we know about what it takes to build relationships. But shouldn't selling be about creating new relationships with customers, clients and patients? No one likes to be pushed and no one wants to talk to someone whose only agenda is to get what they want. By not focusing on the sale, but on building trust instead with your potential clients, you can eliminate angst, negativity and frustration, and watch your sales grow to levels you never thought were possible to achieve.

Have you ever made a sale without trying to? You know what I mean, it just happened naturally without you having to force it to happen. That unconscious process is the same as the process that I have created at the conscious level, giving you a "system" you can follow which makes the sales process effortless.

The Sales "Wake Up" Call That Changed The Sales Game

About thirteen years ago, after spending many years studying the great sales gurus, designing sales training for major companies and completing my Master's degree in Training and Development, I had the most important sales call of my life.

At the time, I was the Sales Manager of a team of 18 at an online software company. One afternoon, I was on the phone doing an online demonstration with the top executives of an account we had been working on for nine months.

The call was going well, extremely well. Everything was going to script – they were interested and asking me tons of questions, and I had all the answers at my fingertips. At the end of the call they thanked me profusely for my time. I still remember the Vice-President's final words: "We'll definitely be getting back to you."

I was so proud of how well things had gone that I could almost feel my head swell as I started to hang up the phone, but

I accidentally hit the phone's mute button instead. They had not hung up, but obviously thought I had, and I could listen to the Vice-President talk to the other executives about our 'oh-so-promising' phone conversation. Here's what they said, word for word: "'Okay, so we're definitely not going to go with him. But keep stringing him along, so we can get more information and strike a better deal with another company."

I was devastated!

My first feeling was outrage – they had lied to me! I felt hurt and used, but the waves of rejection that swept over me were even worse. "I'm a good guy," I told myself. "I did everything right. I've studied all the best sales programs in the world. I didn't cut any corners. Why are they treating me this way?" Then I remembered all the other times that I had gotten a gut feeling that something was 'off', about how a prospect was reacting to me. I could never put my finger on it, yet at some level I knew that everything I had learned was incomplete. I'd ignored that nagging discomfort and kept on doing what I had been doing, until that wake-up call.

A lot of today's sales programs would analyze that call and conclude that if a prospect lies to you, then it's okay to lie back. If they're aggressive to you, it's okay to be aggressive in return (because that's how you control the situation). If they try to box you in, it's okay to force them into a commitment. But this buyer and seller conflict, battle or whatever else you want to call it, just felt so wrong. It took me a long time to figure out one basic truth that none of those 'fight back' sales programs ever talked about – my sales approach was all wrong!

There was something fundamentally wrong with how I was approaching selling – I needed to change. It was at this point that I was finally able to let go of the outrage and rejection and take responsibility for having tried to sell the 'wrong' way. I realized that the old ways of selling had everything backwards, and this freed me to create a new sales approach with a primary focus on creating trust and removing sales pressure from the process.

Ironically, when your mindset is focused on creating trust with your prospects, sales happen naturally, without resistance.

When I think about that life-changing sales call above, I realize that the executives knew I had an agenda for that call – to make them buy what I had to sell. I did it by "the book", dealt with their objections and pushed subtly to move things forward – you know the drill. As it turned out, they were playing along. While at first I took the rejection personally, I later realised that the problem wasn't me, it was the whole dynamic of trying to make the sale.

Did it ever occur to me to think about the ways I could develop a relationship of trust with them, so that we could explore what issues and problems they were trying to solve? No. Did I ever contemplate that by not knowing more about their issues and problems, I didn't know whether I could help them? No. Did it ever occur to me to ask them, "Where do you want to go from here?"

No. I was on that call to make a sale, and the sales pressure I was exerting with every word made them feel it was okay to lead me on and even lie to me. Think about it: would they have lied to me if they had trusted that I wouldn't exert sales pressure on them, regardless of their decision? Probably not.

A big lessoned learned: selling is all about trust. People can sense when you are more concerned about your commission than with their best interests. When you treat people as people, not as prospects, and reveal your trustworthiness, they will start to trust you. They will see you as a problem solver, focused solely on their needs. From there you have the basis of a long-term relationship – the true competitive advantage in this new economy.

Your *new* focus is to take the pressure out of the conversation to help both parties get to the truth of whether you're a fit or not together...ironically, that makes more sales!

That's why I named my trust-based sales system: Unlock The Game®, to essentially unlock the chasing game that everybody hates so much and to help people become more successful by efficiently and authentically, getting to your prospect's truth.

If you look at most company's sales pipelines, you'll see they are measuring their sales consultants based on certain behaviors – how many initial calls they make, how many follow-up calls they do, or how many surveys they send out.

But, in reality, that's the *wrong* measurement.

The real measurement should be, how effective they were at getting to the *truth* of their potential client (what's *really* on their mind), so they're not playing the chasing game and keep pushing more numbers through their pipeline.

Debunking The Sales Myths

Before you begin to dig into the core content of this book, to set the stage of my sales mindset and philosophy, now shared by thousands of businesses worldwide, I'd like to debunk a few common sales myths that are probably still wedged in the back of your mind, ultimately holding you back from your true sales potential.

Myth #1: Sales Is A Numbers Game

Of course I know you've heard that one before many times and it's probably still part of the way you might think the sales game is played.

Guess where the "numbers game" concept came from? That notion came from a sales consultant making a phone call, getting rejected, and their manager said, "Just make more calls."

It's supposed to be about how many calls you make and how many contacts you reach, right?

Well I'm going to challenge you on that belief system. In this new economy, with trust being at its lowest point than it ever has been in the marketplace, it's no longer about how many calls you make or how many contacts you reach -- *it's about how deep you go on each conversation.*

It's about how good you are at creating trust. It's about how good you are at making a human connection in a conversation, so you can quickly and efficiently find out if it's a fit or not between you and your prospect.

That is the new sales mindset rather than focusing on how many contacts you make and how many leads you burn through.

Myth #2: The Sale Is Lost At The End Of The Process

You can probably relate to spending a lot of time with a potential prospect in your sales process. You do everything right, then as you wait for the contract or final approval for the sale to come through – it just doesn't come in as you expected.

Have you had that happen to you before?

Can you relate to a situation like that? Here's what's important to realize, in this new economy, the sale is no longer lost at the end of the process, it's now lost at the *beginning* of the process.

It's actually lost at, "Hello". I'll prove it to you right now.

Let's say someone calls your office and says to you, "Hi, my name is... I'm with... we are a..." What goes through your mind in about three seconds?

Classic sales pitch, right?

It's over at "hello", isn't it?

It's time to evolve beyond the "numbers game" and focus on going deep into your conversations so you create authentic trust with your potential clients.

Usually when that experience happens, you start to blame yourself and you might say, "Oh, I didn't close hard enough. I should have closed more aggressively." You start beating yourself up and wondering why you lost the deal at the end of your process.

Myth #3: Rejection Is Part Of The Sales Process

You probably don't like rejection, but still may assume it's just an accepted part of the sales process if you want to be successful.

In other words, rejection is something we are supposed to just accept. As business owners, entrepreneurs and sales consultants, we're supposed to accept that we are supposed to be tough and "thick skinned" to not let rejection affect us.

I'm going to directly challenge your thinking on that. We discovered through our many client success stories that rejection is actually *triggered*.

As it turns out, we discovered there are certain triggers that actually cause the other person (your prospect) to put their guard up.

Read on and I'll share with you what some of those triggers are. Imagine what your life would be like if you became aware of those triggers and removed them from your process? This could quickly lead to a major sales breakthrough in your sales results, literally, overnight!

I believe that Unlock The Game is the only sales system in the world that can completely eliminate rejection from your sales process, while at the same time, create an immediate increase in your sales results.

I'd like to now introduce you to the three core principles behind the Unlock The Game mindset and philosophy. I'm also going to walk you through some examples of how to use our trust-based approach in your business to create immediate results.

Core Principle # 1: Always Be Diffusing Pressure

The first principle is about diffusing the hidden sales pressure that resides underneath the sales conversations you have with your potential clients.

Your new goal in your sales process should be to focus only on one thing, and that is focusing on taking the pressure out of your sales conversations to allow the other person to feel comfortable telling you the truth of what's really on their mind.

I'll give you an example of what I mean by using a sample of our proprietary trust-based languaging that we have developed and tested over many years.

(Tip: The languaging you choose to use in your sales conversations, if it's not trust-based, can immediately trigger rejection. Our unique Unlock The Game trust-based languaging, if delivered with the right mindset, never triggers rejection because it's pressure free and doesn't contain a hidden agenda.)

Let's just say for instance, you have a first call with a potential client, a first conversation. You call them or they call you. The call is going well, good conversation is happening and the call is naturally coming to a close.

Typically, what are you supposed to say at the end of a call like that? What would you normally say?

Most likely you might say something to move things forward in your sales process like: "How about we get together or schedule a call to have a next conversation?"

Traditional selling has conditioned us to focus on moving the conversation forward to the "next step", right?

We're supposed to be continually moving things forward in the sales process, because if we aren't doing that, then we feel like we aren't "selling".

But what can happen if you attempt to move things forward in the conversation at the end of a first call like that, but they're not ready to move forward yet?

What can be broken right there?

Yes, you're correct, you risk losing *trust* at the beginning of your process.

You see, our successful clients have learned to NOT try and move things forward in a sales conversation like that.

In fact, our approach avoids triggering momentum towards the sale because that puts subtle pressure on your prospect. In most cases, they can feel your intention is to only move them down *your* sales process closer to a sale.

Let's go back to this sales scenario, using the Unlock The Game mindset and philosophy of focusing on creating trust and getting to the truth, instead of attempting to trigger forward movement towards the sale.

The call is coming naturally to the end of the conversation, instead of saying: "Let's move things forward and schedule a next step", we instead would use our trust-based languaging, here's a sample: "Where do you think we should go from here?" I'll say it again, "Where do you think we should go from here?"

How do you suppose that changes the dynamic of the call?

At first it may feel as if you're losing control of the forward momentum...and that is *exactly* what you want to happen.

What happens almost instantly is this will immediately differentiate you from everybody else offering them a similar solution because you're not using typical momentum-based sales languaging.

They are usually quite pleasantly surprised because they weren't expecting you to be so open to the truth of what they have to say.

Within a split second, in their mind, they will think: "Hang on, this is a question I probably haven't been asked before". And it's going to make them actually think about it and respond with a truthful answer back to you, as opposed to eliciting a standard automatic response.

What you're doing here is actually humanizing the conversation early on in the relationship so they feel that you are truly authentic about your intentions.

You are beginning to unlock *your* sales game so-to-speak, and you are creating trust and differentiating yourself, all at the same time.

And, if they are a fit with you, they themselves may say to you, "How about we move this thing forward and discuss this next week?" They'll move the process forward rather than you.

You'll experience how good it feels to not have to put pressure on them to move them into your process.

(Tip: Another trigger of rejection is the way in which you deliver your trust-based languaging. If it's delivered like a sales script and not in a natural way, then you'll experience push back. But, if you deliver your languaging in a centered and relaxed manner, slowing down your pace, having empathy in your tone, showing you really care about them – you'll create instant and authentic trust.)

It's important that you immerse yourself in our trust-based mindset so you master this approach, so you can avoid rejection forever.

Here's a free 10-part audio seminar for you entitled: "*7 Sales Secrets Even The Sales Gurus Don't Know!*" to learn more of our languaging and to go deeper into our trust-based mindset: *www.UnlockTheGame.com/GuruSecrets*

Core Principle #2: Get To The Truth

Getting to the truth with your prospective clients, what does that exactly mean?

Truth is sometimes an abstract concept.

What it means is allowing the other person to feel totally comfortable telling you exactly what's on their mind -- the truth of what they're actually thinking.

I'll give you an example. Let's say someone calls your office and says to you, "I'm looking at your solution for our company, can you please send me information about your company and your solution?"

The typical reaction to that is, "Sure, what's your address and we'll send it to you right away -- then, we'll give you a call and follow up with you in a few days."

Now, what could be three hidden agendas behind that request?

The first could be they are just shopping you against someone else.

The second is they would prefer not to have a conversation with you.

Third, they really are interested in your solution. (Was that the first agenda you thought of?)

Here's the key point, you don't know what the *truth* is behind their information request. So your new goal is to get to the *truth*, rather than try and move them towards a sale.

How do you do that? Using our mindset and trust-based languaging, you can say: "It might make sense, to first get a good understanding of what your particular issues are you are trying to solve, then I can better understand exactly what to send you, as opposed to sending information that is not customized to your exact needs... does that make sense?"

Now, if you deliver this in a slow and relaxed tone, without any momentum in your voice, what will most likely happen is they will begin to open up about their needs.

This now gives you a chance to listen carefully to their challenges and to re-engage them into a deeper conversation, all the while, creating trust.

Surprisingly, if you are delivering this with our trust-based mindset, what will most likely happen is, you will learn the truth of their situation, create trust with them, and both discuss whether it makes sense to continue the conversation.

And guess what? The original information request will most likely never come up again in the conversation – because you have connected with their needs and now they prefer a conversation with you over receiving information and being chased.

That's an example of getting to the *truth* with a prospective client, rather than chasing the sale.

Core Principle #3: Be an Expert Problem Solver

The third principle is just as important as the first two. This is about shifting your mindset away from using your "sales pitch" at the beginning of your sales process when engaging a new prospect.

So many of the business owners and sales consultants that we work with are so passionate about their solution, the moment they find someone who is remotely qualified to become a client, they immediately default into "pitch" mode.

They want to show the prospect their solution or "demo" as soon as they can, because they assume their solution, on its own, is enough to speed up the sales process.

Read that last paragraph again.

If you find yourself in that mode, that is probably why you are chasing what I call "ghosts". "Ghosts" are prospects who expressed interest in your solution, you showed them and/or talked with them about your solution, they said something like: "Looks interesting, I'll think about it", and now you're stuck chasing them.

Do you have any "ghosts" you are currently chasing?

Here's the reason why this is happening for you. Most likely you believe in what you are selling at a deep level. You are probably even passionate about what you are selling.

So passionate, that the moment you meet someone who has the problem your solution solves, your instinct is to solve their problem with your solution.

Essentially, your self-confidence comes from the expert knowledge of your solution.

But, what if you discovered that the true way to make your sales breakthrough was to know your prospective client's problems better than they do and that your conversations with them at the beginning of your sales process were not about your solution, but were a deep dive into their problems.

This would require you to not just be an expert on your solution, but to be an expert at their problems at a deep level.

When you make that mindset shift to being an expert problem-solver rather than just being an expert at delivering your solution, you create an almost unbreakable bond with your prospect. They begin to see you as the only choice for them, because you understand them, better than they understand themselves.

This topic could be an entire seminar in itself (it actually is!), but for now, I'll leave those thoughts with you to begin thinking about how you can become an expert problem-solver rather than just an expert solution provider.

This has been a fairly long introduction for a reason.

It's important that I help you immerse yourself into our Unlock The Game trust-based mindset in a deep way. Because without making a mindset shift away from traditional sales conditioning, it will be very difficult for you to take your sales results to a completely new level.

The chapters in this book are a compilation of my very best trust-based mindset and languaging articles I have written over the years that have resonated deeply with our subscribers and clients worldwide.

I hope they resonate with you and that you can take and adapt the lessons directly into your sales process and implement them right away to experience your sales breakthrough.

If this book does connect with you and matches your values and personality, I'd love to hear from you personally.

Just send me a message through our "How Can I Help You?" box at www.UnlockTheGame.com.

To your success,

Ari Galper
The World's #1 Authority on Trust-Based Selling
Founder & CEO of Unlock The Game®

Chapter 1

Seven Ways To Cut Loose From Old Sales Thinking

Old Sales Mindset	New Sales Mindset
Always start out with a strong sales pitch.	**Stop the sales pitch. Start a conversation.**
Your goal is always to close the sale.	**Your goal is always to discover whether you and your prospect are a good fit.**
When you lose a sale, it's usually at the end of the sales process.	**When you lose a sale, it's usually at the beginning of the sales process.**
Rejection is a normal part of selling, so get used to it.	**Hidden sales pressure causes rejection. Eliminate sales pressure, and you'll never experience rejection.**
Keep chasing prospects until you get a yes or no.	**Never chase prospects. Instead, get to the truth of whether there's a fit or not.**
When prospects offer objections, challenge and/or counter them.	**When prospects offer objections, validate them and reopen the conversation.**
If prospects challenge the value of your product or service, defend yourself and explain its value.	**Never defend yourself or what you have to offer. This only creates more sales pressure.**

Let's take a closer look at these concepts so that you can begin to open up your current sales thinking and become more effective in your selling efforts.

1. Stop the sales pitch. Start a conversation.

When you call someone, never start out with a mini- presentation about yourself, your company and what you have to offer. Instead, start with a conversational phrase that focuses on a specific problem which your product or service solves. For example, you might say, "I'm just calling to see if you are *open* to some different ideas related to preventing downtime across your computer network?"

Notice that you are not pitching your solution with this opening phrase. Instead, you're addressing a problem that, based on your experience in your field, you believe they might be having. If you don't know what problems your product or service solves, do a little research by asking your current customers why they purchased your solution.

2. Your goal is always to discover whether you and your prospect are a good fit.

If you let go of trying to close the sale or get the appointment, you'll discover that you don't have to take responsibility for moving the sales process forward. By simply focusing your conversation on problems that you can help prospects to solve and not jumping the gun by trying to move the sales process forward, you'll discover that prospects will give you the direction you need.

3. When you lose a sale, it's usually at the beginning of the sales process.

If you think you're losing sales due to mistakes you are making at the end of the process, review how you begin the relationship. Do you start with a pitch?

Do you use traditional sales language, such as: "We have a solution that you really need" or "Others in your industry have bought our solution. You should consider it as well"?

Traditional sales language leads prospects to label you with the negative stereotype of being a "salesperson". This makes it almost impossible for them to relate to you with trust or to have an honest, open conversation about problems they're trying to solve and how you might be able to help them.

4. Hidden sales pressure causes rejection. Eliminate sales pressure and you'll never experience rejection.

Prospects don't trigger rejection, you do – when something you say, and it could be very subtle, triggers a defensive reaction from your prospect.

Yes, something you say. You can eliminate rejection forever simply by giving up the hidden agenda of hoping to make a sale. Instead, be sure that everything you say and do stems from the basic mindset that you're there to help prospects identify and solve their issues.

5. Never chase prospects. Instead, get to the truth of whether there's a fit or not.

Chasing prospects has always been considered normal and necessary, but it's rooted in the macho selling image that, "If you don't keep chasing, you're giving up, which means you're a failure." This is dead wrong.

Instead, ask your prospects if they'd be open to connecting again at a certain time and date so you can both avoid the phone tag game.

6. When prospects offer objections, validate them and reopen the conversation.

Most traditional sales programs spend a lot of time focusing on "overcoming" objections, but these tactics only create more sales pressure.

They also keep you from exploring or learning the truth behind what your prospects are saying. You know that words like "We don't have the budget," "Send me information," or "Call me back in a few months," are polite evasions that are designed to get you off the phone. So stop trying to counter objections. Instead, make a shift to uncover the truth by replying, "That's not a problem."

No matter what the objection, use gentle, dignified language that invites prospects to tell the truth about their situation, without feeling you'll use it to press for a sale.

7. Never defend yourself or what you have to offer. This only creates more sales pressure.

When prospects say, "Why should I choose you over your competition?" your instinctive reaction is to defend your product or service because you believe that you are the best choice and you want to convince them of that. But what goes through their minds at that point?

Something like, "This 'salesperson' is trying to sell me, and I hate feeling as if I'm being sold." Stop defending yourself. In fact, come right out and tell them that you aren't going to try to convince them of anything because that only creates sales pressure. Instead, ask them again about key problems they're trying to solve.

Then explore how your product or service might solve those problems. Give up trying to persuade and let your prospects feel they can choose you without feeling sold.

The sooner you can let go of the traditional sales beliefs that we've all been exposed to, the more quickly you'll feel good about selling again and start seeing better results.

Chapter 2

How To Sell Using Your Right Brain – So You Can Make Selling Enjoyable And Productive

Because the right brain is...	Consider this...
1. Involved in process (not outcome)...	* Before you make a sales call, think to yourself, "My goal is not to make the sale but to create a conversation based on how I can help the other person."
2. Intuitive (not calculating or manipulative)	* Avoid changing who you are when you make your call. There's no need to be on "stage" or to sound enthusiastic. Just be your everyday relaxed self, as if you're calling a friend. People know when you're being genuine and when you're not.
3. Flexible (not linear)	* Throw out your linear sales script and generate a spontaneous conversation based on the problems you can help the other person solve.

**4. Concrete
(not abstract)**

* Develop two or three specific problems that you know your product or service solves.

**5. Holistic
(not compartmentalised)**

* Let go of thinking "buyer-seller" and view the person you're calling as another person, not as a "prospect."

**6. Open-ended
(not rigid)**

* Let go of worrying about driving the conversation "forward". Instead, open your call with a problem statement that generates the response, "What do you mean?" or "Tell me more."

Chapter 3

Seven Steps To "Following-up" Without Pressure

Here are seven important steps to follow:

1. Don't assume the sale.

Prospects are used to the traditional buyer-seller relationship. They assume you'll pressure them and so may not tell you things that could make them vulnerable to pressure. Until you're sure you know the complete truth, you can never assume the sale is yours.

2. Keep making it easy for potential clients to tell you their truth.

Toward the end of your conversation, ask: "Do you have any more questions?" If the answer is no, follow up with the one hundred per cent final truth-gathering question, which is: "Now, are you one hundred per cent sure that there's nothing else that I can do on my end to make you feel more comfortable with this situation?"

You'll be amazed how often people will reply, "Well, actually, there's one more issue..." It's at this point that you really start to hear their truth.

3. Call back to get to the truth, not close the sale.

Most potential clients who suddenly disappear expect you to chase them down. They expect you to call and say, "Hi, I was just wondering where things are at?" Instead, eliminate all of the sales pressure by telling them that you're okay with their decision not to move forward and not call you back. In other words, take a step backwards. Most of the time, this will open the door to a new level of trust-filled communication.

4. Reassure them that you can handle a "no".

Of course, we'd rather hear a "yes". However, the only way to free yourself and your clients from subtle sales pressure is to let them know that it's not about the sale – it's about the best choice for them. If that means no sale, it's okay with you.

5. Ask for feedback.

Whenever prospects disappear, call them back (use e-mail only as a last resort because dialogue is always better). Simply ask, "Would you please share your feedback with me as to how I can improve for next time? I'm committed to understanding where I went wrong." This is not being feeble or weak, it's being humble. This invites the truth.

6. Don't try to "close" a sale.

If your intuition tells you that the sales process isn't going in the direction it should be going (which is always towards greater trust and truth) then trust those feelings.

Make it safe for prospects to tell you where they stand. It's simple: all you have to say is, "Where do you think we should go from here?" But be prepared for their response because you might not want to hear the truth of how they're feeling. You can cope with this by keeping your larger goal in mind, which is always to establish that the two of you have a "fit".

7. Give yourself the last word.

Eliminate the anxiety of waiting for the final call that will tell you whether the sale is going to happen. Instead, schedule a time for getting back to each other during your conversation. This eliminates chasing. Simply suggest, "Can we plan to get back to each other on a day and at a time that works for you? Not to move things towards the sale, but simply to bring closure, regardless of what you decide. I'm okay either way, and that'll save us from having to chase each other."

You'll find that these suggestions make selling much less painful because you stay focused on the truth instead of the sale. The truth is, the more we release the idea of needing to make the sale, the more sales we are likely to achieve.

Chapter 4

Seven Ways To Stop Chasing Decision Makers

Don't despair! Here are seven ways to end the chasing game with decision makers:

1. Understand the psychology of working in an organisation.

No one in an organisation wants to make a wrong decision and then be left holding the bag and looking bad. Even many CEOs of companies can't make final decisions without the other executives on their team buying in.

So, even if your contact tells you that he or she is the only one making the decision, in most cases that's highly unlikely, especially in larger organisations. Once you understand that, you'll find it easier to roll with the news that others are actually involved in signing off on the decision.

2. Make sure your contact has the authority to sign the agreement without getting approval from others.

How many times have you been told: "I'm the decision maker and I decide if we'll purchase your solution or not"? Contacts may say this with total confidence and we usually take them at their word, only to discover later that they didn't want us bypassing them to get to the other decision makers.

Here's how you can avoid this situation: after they tell you they are the decision maker, you simply say in a relaxed, easy-going conversational manner, "Oh, okay. No problem. So, basically you're the only person who signs the agreement, and no one else needs to be involved with this decision?"

It's amazing what happens when you ask this question. First, there's likely to be a short silence, and then all of a sudden you learn that other decision makers are involved. Once you know this, you can rethink your approach.

3. Don't panic when you discover other decision makers are involved.

Don't get thrown off track when you suddenly learn, deep into the sales process, that other decision makers need to be involved in the decision. When this happens, gently suggest that it might make sense to come up with a way to get them involved with the proposal, so they won't be caught off guard.

4. Suggest a conference call to connect with the decision makers.

Suppose you find out that two other decision makers are involved. Now you have a total of three! What can you do to avoid the delay that's inevitable when your contact tells you, "I need to get hold of Mike and Julie, but they're both travelling, so I'll get back to you after I speak with them"?

This situation is often the "black hole" of selling, because you can wait for weeks until your contact finally tracks down Mike and Julie and gets back to you.

Here's how to avoid this. You simply say, "Okay. No problem. Sounds as if Mike and Julie are an important part of the process... I'm wondering if it might make sense to pull together a brief conference call with you all so that they can get an overview of what's happening. That way you can avoid chasing them down and everyone can get up to speed at the same time. Does that make sense?"

The answer you get will tell you a lot about where you really stand. If your contact says, "Sure. That makes sense. Let me schedule it," things are looking good. But if you hear, "Nah, I'll just try and get hold of them when I can and then get back to you," he could be saying, "We aren't really that interested."

5. Work with your main contact to set the agenda for the conference call.

If your contact agrees to the conference call, spend some time working together on a well-thought-out agenda. Emphasize that your main purpose is simply to inform the others about what has happened so far.

It's crucial that you assure your contact that you will in no way apply any type of sales pressure on the other decision makers during the call.

Why is this important? Because many times contacts are reluctant to pull together a call because they're afraid that the salesperson will put the participants on the spot, and that would make things awkward for everyone.

When you begin the call, simply say: "The purpose of our call today is simply to bring you up to speed on what has happened so far, so that you all have the information you need to think this solution through at your own pace. Here at XYZ, we don't believe in pressuring people to make decisions." Your contact will love you for this.

6. Ask your contact to arrange the conference call.

When you suggest a conference call with all the decision makers, it's important to put your contact at ease. Too often, salespeople get anxious and say, "I'd be happy to contact the other folks and schedule the call for a time that works for all of us," but that may make your contact think you're going to try to influence the others before the call.

To avoid accidentally triggering any "sales alarms", simply ask your contact if he or she would be open to coordinating the call, by saying: "It might make sense if you could e-mail them to coordinate a time for all of us to connect, since you're closer to them than I would be."

7. Get to the truth about where the deal stands.

So you have the conference call and you feel it went well, with lots of good discussion. Your intuition is telling you that everyone seemed positive about your solution.

Now you want to find out the truth about where the deal stands, but you need to be careful not to call your contact and put subtle pressure on him or her to give you a final answer.

You want to get that answer without asking outright, but you can't until you've uncovered the truth about where everyone stands. When you call your contact back, don't use the tired old phrase, "I'm just calling to follow up." That just kicks off sales pressure. Instead, say, "I'm just giving you a call to see what kinds of questions the others on the call might have, since those types of calls don't always address everyone's issues or concerns." This will allow your contact to talk about where he or she stands and you can then ask, "Where do you think we should go from here?"

These seven tips will help you put an end to the dreaded game of chasing decision makers.

Chapter 5

How To Recognise And Diffuse Hidden Pressures In Selling

Here are four hidden sales pressure points to be aware of:

1. Focusing on the sale

If you're like most people who make sales calls, you're hoping to make a sale – or at least an appointment – before you even pick up the phone. The problem is the people you call somehow almost immediately notice your mindset. They sense that you are only focused on your goals and interests, rather than on finding out what they might need or want. This short-circuits the whole process of communication and trust building.

So try this. Practice shifting your mental focus into thinking, "When I make this call, first I'm going to build a conversation. From this, a level of trust can emerge which allows us to exchange information back and forth. And then we can both determine if there's a fit or not." When your focus shifts from making a sale into making a conversation, there's no sales pressure. Many people enjoy conversations. Moreover, as long as you're sincere, this will be one of them.

You're also exchanging information rather than "informing" someone of your product or service. This helps your potential client know that he or she matters to you. This means you're not being seen as "pushy".

Keep in mind that letting go of trying to force the outcome of the conversation into a sales event means you are totally relaxed with the idea that your solution may not be a fit for them. When you're exploring right along with another person whether there's a "fit", then that person feels no sales pressure.

2. Talking about ourselves first

When we start our sales calls with a mini-pitch about who we are and what we have to offer, we've introduced sales pressure right away. The other person senses that all we care about is the sale and not them.

So, instead, start your conversation by focusing on a need or issue that you know the other person is likely to be facing. Step into their world and invite them to share whether they're open to exploring possible solutions with you.

3. Forcing the conversation into a pre-planned strategy or script

Here's a hard one to avoid if we're using scripts or carefully planned selling strategies. When we rely on these methods, it's usually because we just don't know how else to "do" selling. However, when we take charge of a conversation in this way, the other person almost always feels like they are being maneuvered. That's pressure.

If we aren't allowing someone else to be fully involved in the conversation, then we're using sales pressure to try to control the outcome. Potential clients feel this sales pressure, even when it's subtle. Therefore, once again, "The Wall" goes up.

I'm not suggesting that we don't prepare and plan for our sales calls. There are some really good ways to begin sales calls that we'll want to use over and over again. Additionally, there are special phrases that we can use which convey well the fact that we're interested in solving a problem for the other person.

What we want to avoid, however, is trying to control a selling conversation. This almost always happens with scripts and old-style sales strategies. Potential clients feel this pressure and respond negatively.

4. Over enthusiasm

The problem with over enthusiasm in our selling is that the other person has to make a decision whether to "buy into" our perspective or reject it. They feel the hidden sales pressure that we want them to be carried along with our enthusiasm. This usually means them breaking, whether gently or abruptly.

With over enthusiasm (which is often just an offshoot of our own tension) potential clients feel somewhat boxed in. They feel the pressure of our expectations and compelled to respond either positively or negatively. Most of them will almost always respond negatively.

Completely eliminating all sales pressure from your selling conversations will certainly invite the other person to respond much more warmly and positively.

Chapter 6

Three Selling Myths To Conquer

Haven't you noticed that the old "tried and true" selling techniques that were once successful in selling have now completely lost their effectiveness?

That's why I've developed a new selling approach that will automatically put you ahead of the game and in a league above your competition quickly.

OLD SALES GURU MYTH # 1
"Selling is a Numbers Game"

When all you know is the traditional way of selling, selling is indeed a numbers game. Yes, you can call people over and over again. You can also chase them until they listen, just so that you go away.

Have you ever wondered how someone came up with the "numbers game" concept? It was really about the rejection we constantly experience when making sales calls. The boss just said to call someone else and so we did. The idea is that if we call a hundred people a day, then we should squeeze out at least a few good leads. However, there's a better and easier way of getting your product or service message across – all in one call.

If you simply change your selling approach, you'll make fewer calls and more sales. How? By engaging in conversations. Yes, that's right. Just talk to people...in your normal tone of voice and without the usual sales pitch approach. When we focus on relationship rather than salesmanship, we will make our sales calls with the anticipation of meeting someone new. We're looking forward to a pleasant conversation to find out whether we can be of service.

The other person subtly but powerfully feels this mindset. You're no longer meeting with defence and resistance right from the start. That will dramatically change the way people respond to your sales calls.

OLD SELLING GURU MYTH # 2
"Use a sales script"

People can tell when you're reading from a script, even if you think you're pretty good at it. There's just nothing personal about a sales script and people pick up on that. Being artificial immediately tags you as a typical salesperson. Therefore, if you can learn to get your message across in a different way, then you'll eliminate the negative triggers that can lose you the sale within seconds.

So, once again, the best way is to begin with a conversation. Anticipate a dialogue, not a monologue. People will respond much more positively. When you allow a conversation to be natural and to "breathe", they know you're present and listening. That feels good to someone who is having to "fend off" salespeople who are really just talking billboards.

OLD SELLING GURU MYTH # 3
"Focus on closing the sale"

Are you "going in for the kill" with your closing sale technique? If you are, you could end up killing your deal instead.

'Old selling' sales techniques do nothing more than pressurise potential clients. They feel like they're being chased. What do most people do when they feel chased? They run! They naturally want to retreat away from that pressure – and that pressure is you.

So learn to avoid the 'push-pull' dynamic between you and the potential client. You'll actually find the sales process moves forward much more naturally (and more often) than when you force things.

In this old myth, if a sale is lost, it's usually at the end of the sales process. The truth is that it's often lost at the beginning of the sales call. When all you're doing is going for a sale, the other person can sense it, no matter how well you think it's camouflaged. When someone senses this sales pressure, "The Wall" goes up and the defenses come out. So stay away from focusing on making the sale. Rather, your goal is always to discover whether you and your potential clients are a good fit.

I can't tell you how useful these new ideas have been in my own life, and in the lives of hundreds of others who have tried them. It's not always easy to shed the old selling myths. Nevertheless, it's worth it. With a little practice, you'll come to a place of actually enjoying your sales calls and getting better results.

Chapter 7

No More Selling Scripts? Five Ways To Be Yourself Again

1. Admit that scripts make you sound "scripted."

When you begin your sales script, prospects detect the very subtle change from your natural voice to your unnatural scripted voice within seconds. "Fine," you might say, "I'll just work on making myself sound natural." But that in itself creates a conflict.

The first step is to realise and admit that you can't "work at" being natural. However, you can let go of your script as a crutch. The idea may sound scary at first because you've been programmed to believe you have to have a script to make a successful sales call. It is possible to learn another way, to make calls without a linear step-by-step script.

2. Start your sales call as a conversation, not a one-way pitch.

If you're used to scripts, you're probably shaking your head and wondering, "How the heck will I know what to say without a script?" You might want to ask yourself why you think you won't know what to say, because the reason for that is important. It means you're basing your call on what you have to offer – and not on what's important to the prospect, because you haven't found that out yet.

Pitching your solution as soon as you begin a call is one of the biggest problems with linear sales scripts because you trigger sales pressure and cause prospects to react with defensiveness or even abrupt, immediate rejection.

Here's another option. Write down two or three core issues or real problems (not benefits or features) that your product or service solves. Then take that "problem statement", as I call it, and put it into words that your prospect can understand. In fact, the wording should be so familiar to your prospects (because it uses the same words as they do every day in their business) that when you start discussing the issue, they'll feel a sense of comfort knowing that your mental focus is on helping them solve their problems and not on making the sale.

3. Create openings rather than forcing a "yes".

'Selling scripts' are linear and step-by-step, so they can move calls in the direction that you want them to go. From the traditional selling point of view, that direction is toward a "yes" because if you don't get a "yes" at the beginning of the sales call, you're not "selling". But that's the biggest problem with scripts. They give you only one path to follow.

If you can start a conversation that triggers a "What do you mean?" response from your prospect, you'll find you can explain yourself in a natural way that creates a two-way dialogue. This lets you learn what you need to find out by flowing with the conversation and without feeling you're getting off-track. Developing your 'problem statement' makes this much easier.

4. Tape-record yourself talking with someone you know. Then record yourself reading your script.

Have you ever heard yourself calling a prospect and reading your script? Probably not. That's why most people who use scripts think they sound natural. They've never heard themselves. But if you do this simple exercise, you'll hear the same kinds of differences that I hear when people role-play with me.

In our day-to-day personal relationships, we simply want to get to know and communicate with others. But when we go into sales situations using scripts, we have an agenda – to make the sale. As scripts trigger this perception, the people you talk with will sense this immediately and put up their guard.

Between our hidden agenda and their reaction, there's no chance to build trust through communication. As we've been taught for so long that we have to control the process, we never stop to think that scripts make it impossible for us to be flexible in how we communicate and build trust.

5. Set a new goal for your calls. Focus on simply opening the conversation rather than trying to control it, so that prospects will feel comfortable telling you the truth about their situation.

Does surrendering your use of a script seem scary? If so, try this alternative and see how it feels. Begin the conversation with, "Hi, maybe you can help me out for a moment..." Most people will respond with something like, "Sure, how can I help?" You can say, "I'm just calling to see if... (problem statement)," which makes it easy for the prospect to reply, "What do you mean?" or "Tell me more." After that, the conversation will flow and the possibilities are endless.

What do I mean by this? If you target their issues, create a conversation around the problems or issues you know they're facing, and explain how your solution solves those problems, you will make great strides. In a conversation that is completely void of sales pressure, prospects will share their truth with you. They'll tell you whether solving the issue is a priority, if they have the resources to commit to it, and everything else you need to know.

When you let go of a linear script, you'll find that you no longer fumble for words if prospects get 'off track' by taking the conversation away from your sales process and into their buying process. In fact, that's exactly what you hope they'll do, because that means they're telling you the truth.

Now that you understand why linear step-by-step scripts create the negative "salesperson" stereotype by making it impossible for you to be your natural self, you can begin learning how to engage total strangers on the phone in ways that make your conversations feel as comfortable as calling a friend. Yes, it's possible, and don't let anyone tell you it's not.

Chapter 8

How To Use E-Mail "Sales Calls" Without Falling Into The SPAM Trap!

This e-mail is a real example that one of my coaching clients sent to me for comments and suggestions:

Dear John,

My name is Michael Johnson and I am with XYZ company. We are the leading provider in back-office operations software with many clients, such as XXX, YYY and ZZZ.

I'm writing to you to see if you or your company would be interested in a demonstration of our software. It would be a brief fifteen to thirty-minute demonstration that we could do at your convenience.

Our website, dogandponyshow.com, lists many testimonials from customers that describe how we have improved their productivity, as well as complete details about our products and services.

I'll give you a call later in the week to see if we can set up a time for the demonstration.

Sincerely, Michael Johnson
Productivity Consultant
XYZ Software

Does this 'sales e-mail' sound familiar? On the surface it looks innocent enough, but take a moment and ask yourself what your instant reaction would be if it arrived in your e-mail box.

The problem is that this message violates the core principles of the Unlock The Game™ mindset by creating the impression that the sender's only concern is making a sale. How?

Let's look at it sentence by sentence

Dear John,

My name is Michael Johnson and I am with XYZ company. (**Starting a conversation without asking a question can be perceived as an intrusion. Also, starting out with "My" and using "I" immediately focuses the conversation on you, not on your prospect.**)

We are the leading provider in back-office operations software with many clients, such as XXX, YYY and ZZZ. (**This sentence is a mini-presentation designed to show off your client list. The writer is assuming that the prospect is already interested in the sender's software. He's also assuming that the prospect has a problem to be solved and that his company's product can solve it.**)

I'm writing to you to see if you or your company would be interested in a demonstration of our software. It would be a brief fifteen to thirty-minute demonstration that we could do at your convenience. (**Offering to demonstrate a solution without first determining any problem is likely to set off negative sales alarms.**)

Our website, dogandponyshow.com, lists many testimonials from customers that describe how we have improved their productivity, as well as complete details about our products and services. (**This paragraph continues the barrage of information, all based on the assumption that the reader is interested. If he isn't, however, this writer has come across as a typical "salesperson". He has communicated that he and his company are aggressive and interested only in the sale, rather than in taking the time to build trust and get to know the issues and problems that face potential customers.**)

I'll give you a call later in the week to see if we can set up a time for the demonstration. (**This is the usual "assumptive" close used by most traditional salespeople. However, it only reinforces the view that this e-mail is an obvious attempt to get an appointment so that the sender can make a sale, rather than opening the communication so they can understand the reader's world.**)

Sincerely, (**This traditional closing is cold and aloof.**)

Michael Johnson
Productivity Consultant
XYZ Software

My comments (in bold) zero in on the specific wording and phrases in the e-mail that feed the negative sales stereotype by giving the impression that the writer cares only about the sale.

The problem is – even if your intentions are honest and sincere – e-mails like this are more likely to burn bridges than to build trust.

There is a better way. Here's the same e-mail, but rewritten from the Unlock The Game™ mindset.

My comments show the reasons behind the phrases and why they both reduce potential sales tension and increase the chances of a favourable response.

Dear John,

Not sure if you can help me, but thought you could possibly point me in the right direction.

(By starting off from a position of humility, rather than with the typical assumptive introduction, and by asking for help, this e-mail gives the reader a chance to either tell the sender that he has reached the right person or to refer him on to someone else.)

Would you happen to know who in your organisation would be responsible for diagnosing and solving productivity issues related to your technology infrastructure – specifically, under-performing servers, outdated software upgrades or out-of-date computer hardware? **(Rather than offering solutions, the writer is addressing some very real problems and issues that may exist in the reader's company. In other words, the e-mail is about the receiver, not the sender. Also, the writer doesn't mention any demonstration because the problems must always come first, and the solutions later.)**

I'm with XYZ company and we specifically help companies solve these types of issues.

(This reinforces that the writer's company solves problems.)

Any help you could provide would be very graciously appreciated. (**This statement expresses the warmth of the writer's gratitude in advance.**)

Warmest regards, (**The warmth of this closing humanises the whole communication.**)

Michael Johnson
Productivity Consultant
XYZ Software

How do you think you would react if you received this e-mail?

Chapter 9

Sales Therapy 101: Breaking Your Fear Of Selling

Traditional sales trainers answer questions about selling this way:

"All you have to do is make more phone calls."

"All you have to do is think more positive thoughts."

"Just learn to accept rejection as a normal part of selling."

In other words, "It's your fault that you aren't succeeding in sales." So, how do you overcome your fear of selling?

In my opinion, the solution actually is simple, and it is based on understanding three simple concepts:

1. It's not your fault.

We can't help thinking there's something wrong with us if other people keep telling us that something shouldn't be a problem, but our own inner feelings tell us that we aren't comfortable doing it.

There's a sort of "old boys' club" sales-conditioning mentality prevalent in English-speaking countries, including the US, Canada, the UK, Australia and New Zealand, that says, "I had to suffer to succeed in sales success, so you need to, too!"

This thinking comes from traditional sales programs that continue to be the accepted approach to selling. What you need to understand, though, is that you may fear selling because you have probably been exposed only to traditional selling approaches, which trigger rejection.

These approaches teach us to make sales calls this way: introduce yourself, explain what you do, suggest a benefit to the potential client... and then close your eyes and pray that they won't reply, "Sorry, not interested" or "Sorry, I'm busy".

If you're still using this traditional approach, you probably hear responses like these the moment you stop talking. They're rejections, and what they do is make you feel rejected – and that's reason enough to make you dislike, fear and avoid selling.

How can selling be a positive experience if rejection is the most common response you get?

2. Are your self-perceptions passive or aggressive?

Whenever I chat with people about the fear of selling, they almost always tell me that they're afraid to make sales calls because they don't want to be perceived as "aggressive".

This is another part of the internal battle. People beat themselves up for being too passive and lacking the confidence to make the next call, but they don't want to call for fear of being seen as aggressive.

Here's the good news: there is a middle ground between "aggressive" and passive". It's a place where you can be who you are, while still being extremely effective with selling, without ever experiencing rejection again.

Unlock The Game™ shows you how you can be incredibly effective in selling without triggering rejection from potential clients. Imagine the possibilities (and the income potential).

3. <u>Learn to let your language match your thinking.</u> NB

If you can centre yourself into a place where you can let go of the feeling that you have to go on using traditional selling 'scripts' and behaviours, you'll find yourself spontaneously using language that you would use in a natural conversation.

Using natural words and phrases – speaking exactly the way you would with someone you know – can transform selling into a refreshing and productive experience.

And, as you let go of the old-school selling model, in which your product or service is your only way of generating a phone conversation with a prospect, you'll make the most crucial transition of all: you'll begin thinking of approaching potential prospects not from your perspective, but from theirs.

Chapter 10

Seven Ways To Sell And Retain Your Integrity

1. Focus on getting to the "truth" of your potential client's situation. You may or may not be a fit for each other, so don't focus on the end goal of making the sale as it will only derail the trust-building process. Without trust, you compromise integrity.

2. Eliminate rejection once and for all by setting realistic expectations and avoiding traditional sales behaviours, such as defensiveness, persuasion and over-confidence. If you're not trying to sell, you can't be rejected.

3. Stop 'chasing' potential clients who have no intention of buying. How can you do this? Shift your mindset and boost your truth-seeking skills so that you can quickly, yet graciously, discern whether the two of you are a potential 'fit' or not.

4. Avoid calling people 'prospects' or even thinking about them in that way. People are people and when you label them in your language or your thoughts, you dehumanise them and the sales process. 'Prospect' reinforces the notion that sales is only a 'numbers game'. Train yourself to think about 'potential clients' instead.

5. Take the 'cold' out of your selling. Don't start with, "Hi, my name is... I'm with... We do..." When you begin a conversation by making it about you, instead of about the other person, you immediately cut off the possibility of opening a dialogue. Try the more humble approach of asking, "Maybe you can help me out for a second," and keep in mind that you're really calling to help them solve their problems.

6. Don't try to 'overcome' objections. Instead, determine whether the objection is the client's truth or not. Then you can decide whether to continue to open the conversation.

7. Avoid using 'I' or 'We' in your e-mail communications to potential clients. These words indicate that the focus of your communication is on satisfying your needs, rather than solving their problems. This sets the wrong tone for a potential relationship.

Chapter 11

Seven Pitfalls Of Using Email To Sell

- Are you sending e-mails to prospects instead of calling them?

- Is e-mail your selling medium of choice because it lets you avoid the rejection that you experience when you make real sales calls?

- Do you wait and wait for return e-mails from prospects that will give you the green light to move the sales process forward?

    It is sad but true, that most people who sell for a living nowadays spend eighty per cent of their time trying to communicate with prospects via e-mail instead of actually picking up the phone and speaking with them. Are you one of those people? If so, you aren't alone...but do you understand why you've turned to e-mail instead of personal contact?

I think there are two core reasons that underlie this unfortunate trend:

- **Fear of rejection.** The sheer negative force of anticipating rejection makes people turn to e-mail to generate new prospect relationships because it hurts less to not get a reply than to hear that verbal "no"

- **Getting blocked by gatekeepers and voicemail.** When salespeople don't know how to break through the barriers of gatekeepers and voicemail, they start thinking, "Forget it, it's not worth the aggravation and it takes too much energy. I'll just e-mail instead."

If you're still using e-mail to sell, watch out for these seven pitfalls:

1. Avoid sales pitches. If you feel you must use e-mail to start a new relationship, make sure your message is about the issues and problems you believe your prospect is having. Don't indicate that you're assuming both of you are a match.

2. Stop thinking that e-mail is the best way to get to decision makers. Traditional selling has become so ineffective that salespeople have run out of options for creating conversations, both over the phone and in person. However, it's best to view e-mail as a backup option only, not as a way to create new relationships. Try to use it primarily for sending information and documents *after* you've developed a relationship with a prospect.

3. Remove your company's name from the subject line. Whenever you put your company and solution first, you create the impression that you can't wait to give a presentation about your product and services. Your subject line should be a humble reference to the issues that you may be able to help your prospects solve.

4. Stop conditioning your prospects to hide behind e-mail. When you e-mail prospects, it's easy for them to avoid you by not responding. They will also get used to never picking up the phone and having a conversation with you, especially when they're afraid that, if they show interest in what you have to offer, you'll try to close them. This creates sales pressure – the root of all selling woes. This avoidance becomes a vicious circle. If you learn to create pressure-free conversations, you'll find that you'll start getting phone calls from prospects who aren't afraid to call you.

5. Avoid using e-mail as a crutch for handling sticky sales situations. Are prospects not calling you back? Many salespeople who call me for coaching ask how they can get themselves out of sticky situations with prospects, but the e-mails they've sent have already triggered those prospects into retreating. It's tricky to come up with the correct softening language in an e-mail that will re-open a conversation with a prospect who has decided to close off communication. Direct, person-to-person phone calls or meetings are much easier and more human.

6. Avoid using 'I' and 'we.' When you start an introductory e-mail with 'I' or 'we,' you immediately give the impression that you care only about selling your solution, rather than being open to a conversation that may or may not lead to a mutually beneficial match between what you have to offer and the issues your prospect may be trying to solve. If you can change your sales language to a natural conversation, your prospect will be less likely to stereotype your message as a spam solicitation.

Finally...

7. If you can, stop using sales e-mails altogether. There is a way to renew your confidence and eliminate your reluctance to pick up the phone and have pleasant conversations with potential prospects. Learn a completely new way of working with gatekeepers that will get you past voicemail and to your decision makers, avoiding the rejection and frustration that are inevitable when traditional selling approaches are used.

For all these reasons, you should think of e-mail as your last resort. If you can learn to pick up the phone without fear, start a trusting conversation with a gatekeeper, learn how to go beyond voicemail and find your decision makers, you'll join the many who have made their own personal selling breakthrough.

Chapter 12

Seven Ways To Get To The Truth: When The Sale "Disappears"

Have you been in this situation before?

These suggestions will help:

- **Don't assume the sale.** Potential clients are used to the traditional buyer-seller relationship, so they may decide not to tell you things that might make them vulnerable to you. Until you're sure you know the complete truth, you can never assume the sale.

- **Keep making it easy for potential clients to tell you their truth.** Towards the end of your conversation, ask: "Do you have any more questions?" If potential clients say "no", follow this up with the one hundred per cent final truth-gathering question: "Now, are you one hundred per cent sure that there's nothing else I can do on my end to make you feel more comfortable with this situation?" You'll be amazed how often people then say, "Well, actually, there is one more issue..." And it's at that point that you really start to hear their truth.

- **Call back to get to the truth, not close the sale.** Most potential clients who suddenly 'disappear' will be expecting you to chase them down by calling them and saying,

"Hi, I was just wondering where things are at?" Instead, *eliminate all sales pressure* by telling them that you're okay with their decision not to move forward and not call you back. In other words, take a step backwards. Most of the time, it'll open the door to a new level of open, trusting communication.

- **Reassure potential clients that you can handle a "no".** Of course we'd rather not hear a "no". But the only way to free yourself and your clients from subtle sales pressures is to let them know that it's not about the sale, its about the best choice for them – and if that means no sale, it's okay, because it's ultimately not about you, but about them.

- **Ask for feedback.** Whenever potential clients 'disappear', call them back (e-mail them if you have to, but only as a last resort because dialogue is always better) and simply ask, "Would you please share your feedback with me as to how I can improve for next time? Now that our sales process is over, I'm committed to understanding where I went wrong." This is not feeble or weak, it's being humble, which often triggers the truth.

- **Don't try to 'close' a sale.** If your intuition tells you that the sales process isn't going in the direction it should be going, which is always toward greater trust and truth, trust those feelings. Then, make it safe for potential clients to tell you where they stand. It's simple. All you have to say is, "Where do you think we should go from here?" (But be prepared, as you may not want to hear the truth about how they're feeling. You can cope with this by keeping your larger goal in mind, which is always to establish whether the two of you have a 'fit.')

- **Give yourself the last word.** Eliminate the anxiety of waiting for the final call that will tell you whether the sale is going to happen. Instead, schedule a time for getting back to each other, as this eliminates chasing. Simply suggest, "Can we plan to get back to each other on a day and at a time that works for you – not to close the sale, but to simply bring closure regardless of what you decide. I'm okay either way, and that'll save us from having to chase each other."

You'll find that these suggestions make selling much less painful because, with Unlock The Game™, you learn to focus on the truth, instead of the sale.

Chapter 13

The "Wall Of Defensiveness": Seven Ways To Tear It Down

1. Curb your enthusiasm. This idea always comes as a shock to anyone who's been exposed to the old 'sales gurus' who insist that, "The more enthusiastic you are about what you are selling, the more people will be attracted to your solution". Boy, are they wrong! When you come across as overly enthusiastic, especially when you're on a first call to a new prospect, your attitude immediately triggers sales pressure and tells your prospect, "I'm excited because I just know that you need what I have to offer!" But, in any new situation, that's exactly what you don't know. So try to curb your enthusiasm on initial calls. Otherwise, you're likely to hit the wall.

2. Avoid assuming that you and your prospect are a fit. You may have the 'perfect prospect' – someone with the exact criteria and profile of your ideal customer. However, if your words or tone of voice say, "I know you'll benefit from our service because you fit the exact profile of our customer base", you'll inadvertently set off alarms that will let your prospect associate you with the negative 'salesperson' stereotype. Instead, learn to be humble and avoid making assumptions. Build up trust so that your prospects want to share their true issues with you. Then the two of you can decide, in a natural, evolutionary way, whether you're a match or not.

3. Don't think that you have to have all the answers or you'll 'lose' the sale. So many of us work ourselves into a frenzy before we actually pick up the phone to call someone. Why? We're afraid that if we make a mistake or don't deliver our pitch perfectly, we'll be rejected. But it's okay not to have all the answers. Ever see the TV show "Columbo"? Was he perfect? No. He was human, humble and unassuming, and people trusted him. It's okay not to have all the answers. Needing to have all the answers is a control trip, and when you're with a prospect, you're not in control. The two of you are in a relationship and the more you internalise that realisation, the more comfortable and less frenzied you'll feel. And you'll be surprised when your prospect appreciates you for being just another human being.

4. **Don't try to overcome objections.** Overcoming objections doesn't build trust. Instead, it only associates you with the negative stereotype of a salesperson who has been trained to move the sales process forward at the prospect's expense. When you hear an objection, diffuse it and re-engage the conversation on your prospect's terms.

5. Learn to diffuse sales pressure. Hidden sales pressure is the root of all sales woes. Diffuse it at the beginning of the relationship, and you'll never have to deal with it again. Shift your mindset and change your language so it reflects you being your most natural self. The most sophisticated sales strategies in the world won't make any difference if you don't know how to diffuse the sales pressure that prospects are only too quick to sense – and back away from – in any buyer-seller relationship.

6. View prospects as potential friends, not as sources of commission. If you see dollar signs instead of human beings when you're with prospects, they'll sense your attitude and see those dollar signs in your eyes. Keep your conversations human by always viewing your prospects as people who have potential problems that you can solve.

7. Acknowledging the sales game diffuses the pressure. If you find yourself in a sales situation that puts your relationship with your prospect at risk – for example, a prospect promises to call you back but doesn't – call the 'game'. Call your prospect and say simply and gently that you really don't want the relationship to degenerate into the stereotypical cat-and-mouse sales game. Your message should always be, "Our relationship, not my commission, is my priority."

The bottom line of all this is: you can no longer rely on <u>what</u> you are selling to distinguish yourself, because there's just too much competition out there. Instead, you must focus on <u>how</u> you're selling. That's the only thing that will make you different from everyone else.

Chapter 14

Hidden Sales Pressure: Seven Ways To Make It Go Away

- **Stop carrying the burden of driving the sales process forward**. Try to engage potential clients based on the problems they're facing, rather than on the solution that you're trying to sell, no matter how much you believe in it. Instead of asking questions that are intended to extract information for moving the sales process forward, listen for cues that tell you where potential clients want to take the conversation, so that they feel understood. If you can let your conversation evolve to that point, *they* will move the sales process forward.

- **Watch out for 'sales' type language.** Statements like: "When shall I follow up?", "Can I come by and show you what I have?" and "Do you still want to move forward?" are all examples of language that inevitably triggers sales pressure. Try to imagine that your potential client is a friend. How would your language change? I bet you'd communicate with spontaneous words and phrases that would spring out of you naturally and allow a trusting connection to emerge, in contrast to the 'me' language that is designed to make the sale.

- **Become aware of your inner voice and what it's saying.** So many thoughts run through our mind before we pick up the phone to call a potential client, such as: "I better have all the answers", "I'd better prepare myself for potential rejection" and "I really hope I can get an appointment." These thoughts stem from traditional sales conditioning which taught us that we always have to be prepared for disappointment and frustration. How about changing that inner voice to a more positive one that will not only make it easier for you to engage in conversations, but will decrease your stress level as well? See how you feel when you tell yourself instead:

- "I'm not going to make any assumptions that my product or service is a fit until we both determine whether there's a problem to solve."
- "Not being 'perfect' with a potential client isn't a sign of weakness, but an indication that I'm human too."
- "I don't need to fear rejection because I'll use an approach that won't trigger it."

- **Don't look at sales as a 'game',** but as a mission to help those in need. If you shift the way you think about selling, you'll begin to experience the relief that comes with shedding the burden of the negative sales stereotype.

- **Find new role models.** Look around you for successful people who sell but don't exhibit traditional sales behaviour and thinking. You can learn from their positive examples. Pay attention to how they build trust and dialogue with potential clients in the same way that they would with friends. They always, always, keep their own agendas in check, so that potential clients feel that their own needs – and not the salesperson's commission at the end of the sale – are priority number one.

- **Be open to a new approach.** You may even still hit your sales goals if you stick with traditional sales thinking, but what toll will this take on your self-esteem? And you will never know what opportunities you lost along the way because you exerted subtle sales pressure on potential clients.

- **Find new ways to build trust.** You know how to build trust. You do it all the time in your personal life. So why is it so hard in selling? Because traditional sales thinking only shows you how to outsmart your potential clients and that kind of approach is totally incompatible with building trust.

If you're skeptical about being able to eliminate subtle sales pressure, you're holding yourself back from making a breakthrough in your sales life.

Chapter 15

How To Genuinely Enjoy Selling

1. Focus on helping the other person.

It's against our nature as human beings to create an uncomfortable situation with another person. That's the core reason many of us get that knot in our stomach when we start dialing a sales call.

When we're only focused on making the sale, this is not a natural meeting place for both people. We want the sale, but the other person usually wants us to go away. Being intrusive is not the finest of character traits, and on some level we know it.

So how can we feel good about selling? We change our mindset from getting the sale into being helpful and look at selling as an opportunity to assist.

How can we possibly feel uncomfortable doing that? Helping people is one of the best character traits we possess. When selling is aligned with our very best way of being, it becomes an adventure. We truly want to help people. We feel very good about this and it shows in our voice. People hear it and their response will surprise you.

2. Be honest and truthful.

You're in a very good place when you choose to be truthful in your selling. If you're not trying to fool anyone, you naturally feel better about making the call. You know that you're trustworthy and people respond to you in a positive way.

When you approach a potential client with integrity and common sense, you're more personable and less tense. Being fully honest is one of your better attributes, and it gives you an opportunity to enjoy the interaction rather than being artificial or manipulative.

People do seem to have a sixth sense about integrity. When they feel you can be trusted, you can truly shine as a person, as well as a potential supplier.

3. Be yourself.

Engage people in natural conversation. The more natural you are, the more comfortable you will feel. This makes the other person feel more comfortable as well.

Avoid playing a role, especially reading from a script. Most people can tell when you're using a script. There's nothing personal about it and they pick up on that.

Being artificial puts you in the 'typical salesperson' category, which is exactly the role most of us detest. It doesn't feel authentic and, unless you're a born actor, it makes you feel skittish about selling.

Give yourself permission to follow the rhythm of natural interaction. Allow the conversation to 'breathe'. Let it be the kind of conversation you would have with a friend.

Practice this and it can turn your sales calls into pleasant conversations. This way you may actually look forward to meeting that new person the next time you pick up the phone.

4. Get into the other person's world.

Shift your mindset away from what you have to offer and instead focus on what their problem is.

So many of us have been trained to think about our services and products, that we don't think about the client's point of view. We aren't really interested in their issues and how we can help solve them.

Be interested in their world and their challenges. You'll find this intriguing. Most of us have a natural flair for problem solving. We enjoy 'fixing things'. So find out what's going on with the person you're talking to.

Make sure the solution you have really does 'fix it'. Get rid of any hidden agendas and truly listen. Let them know that you're interested in them and their world.

Move outside your own sales agenda to focus on the needs of others. This makes you a better human being and helps you to leap past the fear of selling.

5. Let go of expectations.

Never assume anything beforehand. Allow the conversation to be one of exploration and discovery, and stay focused on the dialogue, instead of any private agenda.

Determine whether it makes sense to continue the conversation, by truly listening. Never presume your prospect should buy what you have to offer, even when it seems they're a perfect fit.

You are not calling to create a situation that is focused on your personal gain, but on helping the other person. Simply have a conversation to explore whether you can help them in some way. This takes pressure off both of you. You'll be more relaxed and they'll be more honest about where they stand.

Believe me, once you start applying these perspectives it will transform your day-to-day work life. Instead of dreading selling, you'll anticipate the adventure of creating a situation where everybody wins.

Chapter 16

How To End Your Fear Of Selling: Three Steps To Changing Your Mindset About Selling!

1. Focus on relationship rather than salesmanship.

Begin your sales calls with the idea of having a conversation around the other person, rather than around your product or service. Let your whole focus be about whether you can assist the person you're calling.

This allows a conversation to unfold naturally and easily around their needs. It also helps you to be more relaxed around the possibility that your solution really may not be a fit for them at this time.

Who doesn't like the idea of meeting new people, and providing help if we can? When your mindset is in this place, then gracious and easy conversations happen. You aren't all tense about whether a sales call will result in a sale. You're operating out of authenticity. You're being a real person, talking to real people.

Can I be of help to you? You probably wouldn't say these specific words, but it's a mindset that's easy to hold and more easily received by potential clients. They won't feel chased by your sales agenda. They'll be more open to explore things with you, and you'll feel the enjoyment of meeting new people and discovering whether you can help them.

When you focus on building this kind of connection with people, you'll find yourself improving your life in many ways. One is obvious – you'll have better selling conversations. This means you'll find your sales going up, and you'll bring much more professionalism into the actual experience of selling.

2. Focus on dialogue, not monologue.

This new selling mindset is about having a true conversation, not a one-way script. It means genuinely anticipating cordial conversations with new acquaintances.

This has to come from you naturally, so it has to be an authentic conversation. You have to believe yourself that you're calling to see if you can help someone with your product or service.

Once you begin to enjoy the idea of conversing with people and building trust with them, your whole being will shift into this new frame of reference and you will begin to be in a place where the sale itself will not affect your behaviour.

When this happens, your fear of rejection goes way down and your enjoyment of the human connection goes way up.

This is where you become free of the old rules around selling because you're not worried about the selling anymore. You're only concerned with helping the client, regardless of whether you make a sale or not, and that's freedom. It's freedom to be professional and authentic.

If you think of upcoming sales calls in terms of dialogue, rather than monologue, you aren't focused solely on what you might get from the conversation. You're operating out of an honest desire to assist, and this always means having a two-way conversation.

3. Focus on problem solving rather than product selling.

No matter what industry you're in, there must be a need for your product or service or you wouldn't survive very long. So whether you're offering entertainment, bookkeeping, computer programs or anything else, you're fulfilling a particular need.

This new selling mindset focuses on identifying these needs from the perspective of potential clients. Shift your mindset away from what you have to offer and focus instead on what their problem is. Step into their world.

Most of us enjoy problem solving. We like to 'fix things'. So it's easy for us to come from a place of wanting to solve a problem. And that's where we begin our selling conversations: from their point of view, their difficulties and whether we might be of service.

Human nature being what it is, we, as people, enjoy other people. And the more we help them, the more we get feedback that is supportive and positive.

We all want to enjoy our jobs and feel good about what we're doing. One of the major benefits of this new selling mindset is to add credibility and integrity to what we do as professionals. When we humanize the process of selling, we step out of the typical one-sided salesperson persona and that feels really good.

Chapter 17

How To Make Your Selling Problem-Focused

1. Potential clients listen better.

In the old traditional sales mindset, we've been trained that the best way to make a sale is by talking about us, our company, our product and the benefits it can offer to potential clients.

Well, the problem with this approach is that it's all about you. The standard pitch, "I'm so-and-so, I'm with such-and-such, and we do such-and-such…" is about who you are and what you do. The moment the people you're talking with realise that you're making the conversation about you, they tune out and turn off. We all do this in our everyday life when we're confronted by someone who talks on and on about themselves.

2. We avoid the numbers game.

The new selling approach walks away from the 'numbers game'. This is the belief that if you call enough people, some of them will listen to your presentation and some of those who listen will buy.

However, when we focus on solving the other person's problems, we break out of that grim scenario. It's no longer about how many people you call and pitch. It's about your ability to connect and build trust within each one of those calls. This is because you're focusing on something (a problem) that others can immediately relate to, rather than offering a long pitch and rolling the dice, hoping that someone will respond positively.

3. Trust and integrity become part of the process.

Most selling approaches try to slip in the back door by using strategies and techniques designed to 'get the sale' and can be annoying to the potential client.

For example, there's a selling approach that's based around intricate questioning techniques. It's designed to get at potential clients' pain and lead them into a sale. The problem with approaches like this is that the goal is always to get the sale and not find out the truth of whether there's a fit between you and your prospect.

In this new way of selling, we focus on the other person and their problems. We're looking for opportunities to assist and we're doing it with the highest of integrity.

This approach to selling doesn't use influence techniques in any way. It speaks straight to the customer's problems in a non-threatening manner. All you have to do is focus on the truth.

4. Problem solving feels better than selling.

When you follow this new selling approach, you become a problem solver rather than a salesperson. This is the most powerful shift you can make. From this place, you're building trusting conversations. You are speaking to the problems of your prospects, rather than pitching your solution. You are thinking from their perspective and engaging with them in their world.

Most of us like 'fixing things'. There's a greater sense of fulfillment in discovering whether we can help someone fix a problem. We're engaging some of the best character traits we have as people, and that feels good. Our days end with a sense of satisfaction rather than frustration.

These are just a few good reasons why problem-focused selling works best. You'll find opening conversations will become effortless. You will also attract people's attention because you're addressing a specific problem that is of concern to them. Prospects won't look at you as a 'salesperson'. You'll stand out because most people who sell are trained to just promote their service or product. Moreover, you'll eventually discover an overall sense of ease permeating your selling day.

Chapter 18

Should You Use A Letter Before Your Sales Call?

Here are four reasons to consider making sales calls without referring to a sales letter:

1. You get pegged as a traditional salesperson right away.

When you start your sales call by referring to a sales letter, you're following a traditional sale and marketing technique. This indicates to potential clients that you're a traditional salesperson.

Do you really want to be associated with something that brings up painful memories of sales pressure? Better to break out of that negative salesperson stereotype entirely and offer something new.

2. People just don't read letters all that much.

You hope that potential clients will have seen your letter before you call them. From among all the other letters that have arrived on their desk, you hope they've read yours (which is unlikely) and remembered it (even more unlikely).

The idea is that when you call, they already know what the call is about. However, almost no one reads sales letters. If they do, they only remember them vaguely.

3. Selling conversations are harder to initiate.

Most people take it for granted that it makes sense to send out a letter before selling. They think this gives them something to start speaking about. They can then say, "I sent you a letter. Did you get that?"

Nevertheless, when you call, these are the reactions you typically get:

- What letter/e-mail?
- What was it about?
- Sorry, I don't remember seeing it. What are you selling?

You may as well not have sent out the letter at all. Saying, "Hi, I'm just calling to see if you got my letter?" does nothing to move the conversation forward or to generate a two-way dialogue. You're still at square one.

4. A letter makes you talk about yourself first.

When you start your sales call by explaining what a sales letter was about, you're talking about yourself, your product and your company. This is exactly what we're trying to avoid in the new selling mindset. We want to talk about how to solve their problems first, not about what we're selling.

Isn't it true that sales letters, brochures and e-mails focus entirely on your company and your product or service, rather than on solving a particular client's specific, individual problems? So it's essentially just an advertisement that you're referring to. Moreover, you've now lost the opportunity to be seen by your potential client as a problem solver. You're just another salesperson who's only interested in making a sale.

Chapter 19

Make Fewer Sales Calls And Get Better Results

1. Rip up your sales script and start a conversation.

If you've been selling for a while, you'll have probably used a sales script. Perhaps using a script is the only way you know how to start a sales call.

But people can almost always tell when you're reading from a script, even if you think you're pretty good at it. There's just nothing personal about it, and people pick up on that.

A script isn't a conversation. It's a linear process designed to move the other person toward a sale. You're not having a real dialogue when you're using a script. So nothing is 'real' about the whole encounter.

A conversation, on the other hand, is a living, breathing relationship. You're two real people, talking normally and naturally. So when you're just being yourself, the other person's walls can come down because you're not coming at them with a one-way sales strategy. So your sales calls typically last longer. You'll make fewer calls and have better results.

2. From 'dreaded salesperson' to trusted advisor.

The old selling strategies teach you to polarise the roles of buyer and seller. You're trying to coax 'prospects' into buying your product.

You're not thinking about their world – their budget, problems or time constraints. You've been taught to think about the sale.

Well, suppose you were to focus instead on the things that matter to the other person. Their problems, for example. What if you were to become a problem solver?

That's exactly the place you want to be when making your sales calls. Imagine approaching someone with the idea of finding out whether you can help them to solve a problem. Imagine the kind of attitude this would convey to the other person.

You're no longer trying to persuade. You're not even thinking about the sale. You're thinking about whether you can help someone solve a problem. You're relaxed, comfortable and authentic.

When you make your sales calls this way, you'll find that others will engage you more. And you'll also be able to really enjoy what you're doing.

3. Gain the respect you deserve – stop pushing and chasing.

The old-school sales gurus essentially teach the same approach. "Focus on closing the sale. Keep pushing forward. Overcome objections. Your job is to turn every no into a yes."

Persuading and coaxing has always been considered a normal and necessary part of selling. But it's rooted in a kind of macho selling image: if you don't keep pushing, it means you're giving up. So you keep trying to move things forward, and you keep 'chasing' with follow-up calls.

Even when your focus is on solving a problem for the other person, you can be coaxing and cajoling. But if you do this, how can you become the trusted advisor I spoke about earlier?

It's really simple. Just let go of your attachment to the sale. When you do this, you can relax into being the professional that you are.

When you stop focusing on getting the sale, you can become a trusted resource. You're no longer chasing, pushing and cajoling. You're helping and that makes a world of difference to people and how they respond to you.

Follow these guidelines and selling can become surprisingly enjoyable. You'll find yourself spending much more time with each person. You'll also see more positive results, whether or not a sale unfolds. Others will tend to respond to you more graciously and your whole selling experience can become a pleasant one.

Chapter 20

Three Selling Mistakes That Trigger Rejection

Mistake #1: Centre the conversation around yourself and what you have to offer.

In the old approach, you introduce yourself, explain what you do and suggest a benefit or feature of your product. And then you close your eyes and pray that the other person will be interested.

Unfortunately, the moment you stop talking you usually hear, "Sorry, I'm busy," or "Sorry, I'm not interested."

You see, you've started your sales call by talking about your world and what you have to offer. But realistically, most people aren't all that interested in you. When you talk about your company and your product, it's just another advertisement to them. You haven't engaged them, so they often just 'turn the page.' Prospects are much more interested in themselves and what's important to them. If you start the conversation by focusing on their world, they're more likely to interact with you. So, instead, talk about an issue or problem they may need solving. Focus on them rather than on what you have to offer and see where it takes you.

Mistake #2: Be confident they should buy your product or service.

In the old selling mindset, you're taught to focus on the sale and be completely confident that what you're offering is something the other person should buy.

The problem with this approach is that you haven't asked them to determine this along with you. So think about it. In the old mindset, you're really deciding for someone else what's good for them. I know this isn't intended, but that's exactly what comes across to your prospects.

So, rather than being full of confidence and enthusiasm, stop for a minute and think about the other individual. Relax into a real conversation instead of moving into a persuasive strategy or sales pitch. Put yourself in their shoes and invite them to explore along with you whether what you have to offer is a match for them.

Others really can distinguish the difference. You're inviting them to see if you might be able to help them solve a problem. This makes for a much better connection right at the beginning, and you'll get that immediate rejection reaction much less.

Mistake #3: When someone brings up an objection, try to overcome it.

You know, one of the reasons why selling is so difficult is that sometimes you are not very familiar with the other person and their business. When you make that first call, you don't know very much about their issues, problems, budget and time constraints.

Chances are, not everyone is going to benefit from your product or service.

So realistically, your company or product isn't going to be a match for everyone. And yet, when someone brings up an objection ("We don't have the budget for that," etc), the old selling mindset trains you to 'overcome,' 'bypass' or 'override'.

But when you do that, you put the other person on the defensive. Something they've said is being dismissed, and here's where rejection can happen very suddenly.

So it's much better to listen to their concerns and continue to explore whether what you're offering makes sense to them. There are some wonderful phrases you can use that validate their viewpoint without closing the conversation.

So now that you've discovered the three major selling mistakes people often make, see if you can shift away from those old self-sabotaging mindsets. When you do, you'll notice that people will engage you much more and the immediate rejection you've grown so accustomed to will happen much less.

Frequently Asked Questions

How long has Unlock The Game been available and how many people are using it?

The Unlock The Game Trust-Based Sales System has been available for over a decade and is being successfully used by thousands of entrepreneurs, business owners and sales people in over 34 countries in virtually every industry.

How is Unlock The Game different from all the other sales programs on the market today?

It doesn't compare at any level. It's completely different because it addresses the hidden psychological roadblocks that hold you back from unlocking your true sales potential. It gives you an easy-to-use new trust-based sales mindset backed by trust-based words and phrases that create real genuine trust with your potential clients. You'll experience an instant sales breakthrough the moment you begin implementing any of the trust-based sales strategies found in the program.

How do I know that Unlock The Game doesn't just contain the same old "sales messages" that I've heard so many times over the years?

Unlock The Game overturns the very definition of what selling is all about. It directly challenges every traditional sales tactic you've been exposed to by the traditional "sales gurus" (you know who they are!).

Will Unlock The Game give me immediate results, or is it a program that I have to study or memorize?

With Unlock The Game, you never memorize anything. Unlock The Game helps you draw upon your natural skills in human communication to create spontaneous, positive conversations with prospects that develop into trusting business relationships based on your ability to solve their problems. The moment you listen to the audios, read the quick and easy materials, you'll begin to experience new breakthroughs that will help you experience instant results.

Does Unlock The Game work with Voicemail and Gatekeepers?

Oh yes, very much so, but not in the way you might think. The sales "gurus" have trained us to try to get "past" gatekeepers, but that creates an inherent conflict because, as you probably know, it's a gatekeeper's job to block you. With Unlock The Game you'll be given immediate trust-based relationship-building strategies to connect with gatekeepers as people who are willing to help you get to where you need to go. And wait till you hear about new ways of handling voicemail!

How do I learn more about my options of learning Unlock The Game?

Visit www.UnlockTheGame.com/GuruSecrets for a FREE downloadable audio seminar or visit www.UnlockTheGame.com to order one of our programs.

How To Work Directly With Ari...

Here are some ways you can have Ari personally take your sales success to the next level.

Private One-on-One VIP Mentorship Day With Ari...

If you're the kind of person who is absolutely committed, without hesitation, to investing in yourself and your business a top priority and you want to be personally mentored by the **World's #1 Authority On Trust-Based Selling**, then this is your chance to spend an entire day with Ari one-on-one. An application is required to be considered for a **Private VIP Mentorship Day** held in sunny Sydney, Australia (or at your location, additional fees apply). In a single day, you will experience the <u>once-in-a lifetime</u> sales and business breakthroughs that you have been searching for. Many of Ari's private clients have flown in from all over the world to spend a day with him and they have all taken with them <u>the exact breakthrough tools, strategies and plans to finally reach their personal and professional financial</u> goals. Inquire for availability by contacting us at <u>www.UnlockTheGame.com</u>

Keynote Speaking At Your Sales Conference, Industry Conference Or Company Sales Meeting...

How many speakers have you heard who were truly memorable? What was special about them? <u>You remember their message resonated with you so much that it changed your life and you'll never forget it.</u> Unlock The Game founder Ari Galper's fresh, original, and inspiring talks and workshops create instant results and inspires them to rethink how they are selling from a trust-based selling point-of-view.

Ari will help your group:

- Understand how traditional "selling" behaviours and "salesperson" stereotypes create sales pressure, frustration, and rejection -- and learn to eliminate these stereotypes forever
- Unlock their inherent sales potential to create trust and open communication with potential clients
- Diffuse any discomfort they may feel about presenting themselves and their products or services to potential clients

If you'd like to have Ari speak to your group, contact us at www.UnlockTheGame.com

On-Site Sales Breakthrough Team Training And Transformation By Ari...

If you'd like Ari to personally come into your company and train and transform your sales team and culture to one of frictionless sales results based on creating deep trust with your prospects, then contact us at www.UnlockTheGame.com.

Success Stories

Ari, with just one simple change in my sales calls you helped me get to the truth with my prospects! I can't stop thinking about everything you have taught me. All the ideas I'm learning I'm implementing right away and it's already saving me time and earning me more trust with my clients. I've been struggling to find a sales approach that is natural and authentic and I'm so happy I've found you. Who would have ever thought that I could be my natural self without being a "salesperson" and increase my sales! Brilliant work and anyone who is selling and has not attended your training is climbing a hill going nowhere fast!" – *Michelle Puch*

"I'm absolutely loving your program Ari! I had a VP of Marketing today say to me, "I have a meeting to run to but, tell me about your new ideas so I can direct you to the right person or have you call back."

I followed your Unlock The Game methodology exactly as you taught me. He then told me someone else would be the best person to handle that type of marketing and transferred me to the decision maker! I would have been "toast" at "hello" without you!" – *John Reisinger*

"A few months ago I signed up for Unlock The Game. The strategies, mindset and new ideas I've learned is no doubt worth at least 10 times more than what I paid. I'm experiencing tremendous success especially with emails, believe or not, I'm closing a lot through email. I know this is a cold way to close a sale, but email is key for me. All and all, with the trust-based strategies that you teach…I can say that at least 50% of the people who email me, buy. That's a very high conversion rate. Thank you Ari!" – *Antonio Moreno*

"Last week I had another breakthrough as a result of your Unlock The Game strategies. I sell advertising and I called a Chiropractic clinic using your sales mindset and phraseology, and then took it a step further: I told the gentleman that answered the phone that I knew that the doctors relied on him to screen out sales calls that would waste their time. I went on to say that I was just calling to see if the doctors would be open to some new ideas related to identifying and drawing in more patients/clients. I unlocked the gatekeeper's game, and brought honesty into the transaction.

The "gatekeeper" ended up talking to me for ten minutes! And then, as the conversation ended, I figured out that the "gatekeeper" was none other than one of the doctors – he had answered the phones to help out on a busy day. He did not tell me that, but it was clear by his answers to my questions and his obvious authority. So, I was able to engage a decision–maker because I showed respect for the gatekeeper instead of trying to sneak past. – *Mike Simpson*

"The minute I got my hands on your strategies, Ari, I devoured everything. I have been in the sales field for 20 plus years and have always had this (Ari) mindset to put the spot light on the people that I am talking with instead of myself, that I'm a servant to assist them and it doesn't have anything to do with me as it's all about them. Unlock The Game has brought me into a clear focus and it's been a great for me and my team. In a two-week period this has totally transformed our business into what we knew it could be. – *Bruce Snider*

"Ari, I started calls yesterday and had my first substantive conversation in years, which ended with the prospect (a good one!) inviting me to an appointment! Your program is fantastic. If I only had this at the beginning of my career, I would have saved me endless hours of dialing for dollars and rejection. Who ever would have figured out (other than you) that there is a more humane way of selling that doesn't sacrifice your soul. The results from Unlock The Game have come so quick, I'm just sitting back loving this process. Thank you, Ari, for this gift." – *Jeff Pawlik*

"Wow, your program is amazing! I have potential clients THANKING me now for calling them because they can tell that I am genuine and care about solving their problem. What you have done is fundamentally changed the sales game, flipped it on its head and given us the keys to finally say goodbye to all the old school behaviors that gives sales such a bad name. Your Mindset and languaging is nothing short of magical. Who would have thought that all these years of thinking that "sales is a numbers game" and it's "all about the close" was all BS brainwashing from the old sales gurus. You are the only one who has actually created a system of trust for the rest of us who want to make lot's of money selling without having to sacrifice our souls! Ari, you're the best!"– *Michelle Finnegan–Nixon*

 "Let me bottom line this for you Ari. I'm an independent marketing consultant and I'm responsible for a 100% of my own revenue generation. I recently presented my services to a potential client as I normally would. Of course, I was exactly what you taught me and by the end of our meeting, a major shift happened. As we were finishing our meeting, he asked "So what's the next step for us to explore working together?"

I continue to use the exact languaging that you suggested in your training and here is what he told me "You know, you're the first Marketing Consultant we've talked to that didn't immediately want to write a proposal and get us to sign it as fast possible. I really respect your candor.

And without skipping another beat, he took out his diary and asked ME for the follow–up meeting to keep the dialog going. Your trust-based selling program is the "missing link" in selling, and the way you weave trust and integrity into the process is completely unique." – *Larry Richard*

"I made two sales today following exactly what I learned from your training! Once the prospect heard the price of our services, he said "that is pretty pricey" and I was very relaxed and real and said "Mr. Prospect you are right and if you do not feel this will be of value to you and your company then maybe we should wait on moving forward until you are 100% confident this will be a benefit to you?" His attitude completely changed, he said "so how do I get started, what do you need from me?" I truly believe that I would have not closed those deals if I used my old way of selling. I have a lot to learn from you, Ari, and I can't wait to learn more!" – *Breanna Hogan*

"Hands down, your Unlock The Game trust-based selling system is revolutionary. I only wish I had my hands on this in the early days. Everyone is so sick and tired of the old sales techniques, especially the notion of putting pressure on someone else to try and make the sale. Ari, you have a true gift of trust-based languaging that I have never seen before. I started implementing what you taught me and was immediately taken by your authenticity and ability to connect in a sales environment. For me, you broke down, step-by-step everything. I had no idea there were certain things I was doing causing my prospective clients not to tell me the truth. Your principles of truth and authenticity along with problem-solving is totally unique. I'm just so glad I found you before I made my next sales call!" – *Christian Marquez*

"This absolutely works. I love the way you present your approach especially after 29 long years of being exposed to the likes of Tom Hopkins, Brian Tracy, Zig Ziglar and all the rest of the gang. Ari's approach hands down beats them all. I have been so much pride now it what I do. This has given me a new lease on life and I've never felt so centered in my sales approach. This has been a breath of fresh air and I only wish this was around 29 years ago, it would have saved me a lot of grey hairs!" – *Roger Simpson*

"Ari, you're the only sales guru bloke that really can teach us a good lesson on how to change our selling approach. My results have been outstanding since your training. It's your mindset that makes it so powerful. What's fascinating is that your approach is exactly the opposite of what all the other sales trainers teach, and that's what makes it so intriguing. I've cleaned up my pipeline, my sales are up and the dreaded chasing game is finally over." – *Ian Kershaw*

"The biggest impact from your program is your unique mindset and how it's the complete opposite of just another "sales technique". I am new to selling, however I have sat across the table from many sales people and know how uncomfortable it gets when someone is "selling at you." I called one company this week and the receptionist started grilling me about who I was, where I was calling from. I froze as I could feel myself getting tense, but then the mindset kicked in and I was able to understand what I did and what I can do to avoid triggering her defense mechanisms so she didn't pigeon-hole me as just another "sales call." – *Ken Uchida*

"Recently, our company was an exhibitor at a trade show. A week before the show, I started setting appointments for decision makers to come to our booth to meet with me. By using your approach and changing my mindset, I was able to diffuse any pressure over the phone. I was able to open the conversation between us and humanize our initial relationship. At that point, it was easy and comfortable to suggest that we continue our conversation at the tradeshow.

Ari, what I'm about to share with you is something I've never seen in my 8 years of selling. When the people I had talked with arrived at our booth, they looked very unsure of themselves–intimidated, even a bit frightened.

When they said, "I'm here to meet with Scott," I gave them a big smile and reached my hand out and said, "Hi, I'm Scott, nice to finally meet you." I then took them away from the booth and sat them down in a neutral area where there was a grouping of chairs, and simply had a conversation with them, like any of us would with one of our best friends over coffee.

Once they realized that I wasn't there to cram our solution down their throat, I could actually see their physical demeanor change. One man, for example, went from uncertainty and discomfort to being a warm, smiling person who welcomed me into his life. It was something I've never seen in selling before.

And the same thing happened with almost every one of the decision makers who came to meet with me. It was unbelievable.

What also surprised me is how I took "rejection." I have to put "rejection" in quotes because I never felt that I was rejected, because my conversations with these decision makers taught me that we weren't able to help everyone.

I found out within the first 5 minutes whether or not they had a problem and, if they did, whether our solution was a possible right one for them. When I determined that we didn't have a solution to their problem, or that our services just didn't make sense for their company, I felt good, because I wasn't wasting their time, or, more importantly, MINE.

Don't get me wrong—I'd like to be able to help everyone, but that's just not realistic. So, instead of chasing someone for the next 6 months, I felt a sense of relief that we had come to a conclusion, even though our companies were not the right match. I obtained 3 verbal commitments to our services at the show, and I'm confident that we'll be able to help several more companies I met with to lower their expenses as well.

Thanks, Ari, for helping me unlock my sales game! – *Scott Bishop*

"Ari's program has transformed our entire thinking and results as it relates to selling to our prospects and clients. Unlock The Game has revolutionized our business by helping us weed out prospects who have no intention of

buying, and it gets us away from the traditional "salesperson" stereotype that we, especially here in Australia, hate so much. Making more sales without having to sell the old way is the best kept secret around. If you're the least bit skeptical about Ari's program, don't hesitate to call me." – *Taki Moore*

"Ari, I just finished your training and frankly I'm blown away. All I can think of is the knot in my stomach that I always felt when making a sales call. Now it's gone. Your method to end pressure has opened up new doors for me. I've always been stuck between two worlds, working hard to retain my professionalism and to avoid any pressure–filled sales related language. Your way of selling keeps me centered and relaxed. I no longer have to shift into an artificial role when I call someone new. Can't wait for your next training!" – *Matthew Yubas*

"I've started to incorporate your trust-based selling strategies into my daily activities and can say I've already seen great results. I'm not sure why I'm so amazed, but it's incredible the amounts of information I'm getting from my conversations. All the tension is gone. It's like pushing a button and just instantly removing the sales tension that usually is hidden behind a sales conversation." – *Peter Trombetti*

"Ari, I wanted to share with you what has shifted with me over the past 8 weeks since your training. I use to dread picking up the phone to make a call to a potential client. It took every ounce of my energy just to get me up and out of bed to get ready for the office because I dreaded going in with my old mindset of having to 'make the sale'. I felt totally inauthentic with my linear sales pitch. I seriously considered leaving my profession. For the first time in over 8 years I feel FREE from the burden of having to throw my solution down my prospect's throats. My energy level has increased tremendously. I no longer find myself fighting that sales demon inside me. Ari, you have been a huge instrument in my sales transformation." – *Brian J. Beckner*

"I've always had a block against 'selling', which I assumed I'd just have to deal with if I was going to be successful, however uncomfortable and out of integrity with myself it might make me feel. What I learned from you Ari is that I don't have to 'deal with it' at all... the exact concerns I have about having to sell (the sales techniques I deeply object to having used on me, and don't like the idea of using on other people!), are things I don't have to use at all for my business, and would probably end up jeopardizing my success if I did. I've known in theory about keeping the sales process about the person I'm speaking to, and their issues, but somehow I've never quite made the connection between the theory and *how* to apply it without having it feel like just another form of manipulation designed to get that 'all–important sale'.

I feel a lot more relaxed about (and dare I say it, actually looking forward to selling) the inevitable conversations that I'd originally thought would have to be about sales, because they'll be helping me get me back to my core purpose for setting up my business in the first place... how can I help people and make their lives better?! – *Tanja Gardner*

"My sales are up for one profound reason: you have taught me a new sales mindset that gets to the core about how to sell without the awkwardness and rejection experienced by most business professionals. Unlock The Game is exactly what I've been needing for years...a new refreshing approach based on honesty and sincerity. Those are the core values that I've always believed in but could never integrate into my sales and cold calling process until now. – *Benita Sanserino*

"My appointment setting ratio keeps getting better using what you taught me in your training. Your mindset and languaging are truly revolutionary. I've always prided myself in not coming across aggressively in a sales conversation, but I never realised the importance my voice, energy level and the words in order to create trust over the phone. My fear of selling is completely gone. I no longer jump at the chance to make a sale the moment I sense an opening in the conversation. And know the minute I call someone I don't fumble for my words, the call isn't awkward and the conversation is a meaningful one." – *Randy Villa*

"I never thought it would be possible to eliminate the rejection and pain that I experienced when I had to bring in a new client. Your Unlock The Game approach is so different yet makes so much sense, I implemented the ideas and my fear of selling began to melt away. It wasn't because of a new "line" or new "script", it was because your ideas fundamentally shifted the way I viewed how to call on someone without working myself into a frenzy." – *Lason Perkins*

"Ari's program is a complete breakthrough. I mean, I'm leaving voicemails and people are calling me back! I've got every sales book there is on my shelf and I've been through all the sales training programs taught by the 'sales gurus", but nothing comes close to Unlock The Game. Not only has all my selling fear and tension gone away, but I'm actually loving making sales calls. It's such a different mindset to be able to engage people just like they were a friend. And you know what, my personal relationships have gotten stronger because I'm being more myself. Oh, almost forgot, I'm earning more money that I ever could have imagined. If you haven't attended Ari's training, you aren't experiencing the most out of life!" – *Mitch Eichner*

"What I'm discovering with your trust-based selling method, is that my dread of picking up the phone has disappeared, and that was my downfall 99% of the time, as most people in sales can possibly relate. But with this new mindset people on the phone just open up to me, I don't have to push or manipulate and I'm getting great conversations, finally. Setting appointments is now a breeze because as you teach with your Mindset, it's not about the appointment, it's about my ability to build trust, that's the main focus and that's what makes me successful. I only wish I had found your program years ago." – *Derek Hughes*

"What happened over the years? Why has selling become so painful? Well, all I know is now I can go back to being myself again. I always hated being associated with the negative "salesperson" stereotype, you know what I'm talking about. Ari, you have taught me how to "let go" of all those old selling habits that have made me feel like I was intruding on the people I called. Your program has released me from that fear and awkwardness that's always held me back. Bringing trust back into the selling process is one of the most profound ideas I've come across in years. Keep up the good work!" – *Doug Allred*

"This program has shifted my entire way I connect with people. My relationships that I'm forming are much more meaningful when I'm selling, my income keeps going up, and selling gets easier every day. The best thing about your system is that I no longer have a dreadful fear of selling anymore and all that reluctance that comes along with it. Unlock The Game should have been around 20 years ago". – *Michael Page*

"I just got off the phone with my buddy Sam telling him I am truly blown away by your Unlock The Game program. It flips traditional selling on its head and the results are truly amazing. Just today, with the few new skills that I learned from the program, I got a speaking engagement and another large presentation to speak to a group of high level managers. I've been using the phone to sell for years, and now after studying your trust-based system...I realize I was doing the same thing I learned the first year, over and over again. Thank you Ari for giving me a new lease on life, because now I actually enjoy selling." – *Sean McCullogh*

"I used to burn through 50–75 leads each day before I'd get one interested prospect. Not anymore. Now that I've changed my mindset and studied your system, I'm making half the amount of calls and getting more appointments than ever before. I feel much more relaxed and less pressured to get the appointment and I sense that same feeling from the prospect as well. Unlock The Game really does work and your questioning whether it will work for you, then you are on the outside looking in. I always knew that there was a better way to sell and now I have finally found it." – *John De Grave*

"Ari, you have an amazing program. All business owners should attend your training and put it in place. It's so much better than the old school methods of hard sales. You rock, dude. Bottom line is this, I use your methods and they work. People on the other end of the phone line like that I'm helping them and talking with them and not at them. This is a complete breakthrough for me. I just dreaded having to pick up the phone to make that call, and I'm a pretty outgoing guy. It's just that inner voice inside of me that was always getting me ready for battle. It was a real drain of my personal energy to have to face rejection and sales pressure every day. Thanks a million to you for giving us this gift!" – *David Parker*

"I'd pretty much given up on sales right before I learned about your training. After working with Ari's mindset, my objectives changed. They are now to focus on the other person's need first, before mine. That way, both of us get our needs met by me helping them solve a problem, then they feel more comfortable buying my solution. I sleep well at night now because I can connect the dots with why my sales were painfully slow." – *Virginia Lukei*

"Finally, you have taught me how to bring back to life so many of my prospects that have dropped off the face of the earth.

I spend so much of my time chasing prospects who show interest, but when I try to call or email them, they just disappear on me. It feels like I'm being treated as someone less than most other human beings. Your Unlock The Game program basically 'saved my life' when it comes to the dreaded chore of chasing prospects, because I now use the ideas from your training, especially the wording that you recommend and all of a sudden my long-lost prospects are calling me back. Brilliant, I wish I had your program 7 years ago!" – *Peter Chung*

"Ari, your unique sales approach caught my attention the minute I heard about you. What I really like is the calmness and confidence that takes place when the "mindset" is really at work. In the past I've played games with myself and psyched myself up to make sales calls.

Unlock The Game has turned everything around for me. I no longer play the "chasing game" as you say. I'm not stressed at the end of the day and I finally feel natural when I'm making my sales calls, calm and centered. Ari, you are the missing link that will add years to my life!" – *Mike Fisher*

"I just finished training and it has really helped me connect the dots with why my sales seem to be going nowhere. I get through the whole process, even through a couple of appointments, and no sale! The sale was lost at "hello", as you have identified. I'm looking forward to correcting my mindset and having my most successful year ever. Thank you!" – *Marissa Ayala*

"I am loving your program, Ari.

Yesterday I was working with a client over the phone and I would usually just let the client give me the information and give them a quote. This time I simply asked him to tell me about his situation and I would see if we were going to be a good fit for one another. We were a fit, I developed unprecedented trust and got a quality client. I can see the difference in my clients now. I am able to read them and they are honest with me. I am also becoming an even better listener and overall more effective person. This whole process is great. Great job, Ari!" – *Scott Henderson.*

"Ari, your program makes perfect sense. I've known for some time that there was something wrong with the traditional way of selling, but could not seem to get past it. I've spoken to new prospects by phone using your approach and have had good results. My old training taught me to push for the appointment the minute someone expressed interest in my products. By using your approach and asking them what would make them feel comfortable about their situation, I'm cutting down on useless appointments and the dreaded cat and mouse sales game." – *Chris Friedley*

"I've absorbed your training, I liked what I saw and decided that true sales call – knowing nothing but the name of the person at a company – would be a great way to test whether just the 'language" of what you suggest might bring me better results than the techniques and strategies I've been using. I've been finding that I kept having to "defend" the call, which was almost always pleasant enough but didn't engage the other person in a dialogue. In other words, I was getting nowhere fast. So this morning I randomly picked a CFO to call. I used your suggested language verbatim, and it worked EXACTLY as you said it would, no pressure, no rejection and a booked appointment to boot! I can't tell you how relaxed and comfortable the conversation went from start to finish. – *Mark Mixer*

"I always thought it was always about how many dials I made, period. That all changed when I got access to your Unlock The Game training. This year I have made half the amount of calls as I made last year, and am making more money than I ever did. But here's the best part. I'm starting to love what I do again. I measure my days not by how many marks I put on my sheet, but by how many relationships I make and how many problems I can solve in a day. This is a much more sane way to live. Thank you, Ari." – *Mike Obremski*

"Awesome training! Creating an approach that addresses the problem for my client is such an "Aha" for me. I love your consistent message of "always telling the truth." So much of what we learn is about making the sale at all costs, and that is why your approach is so refreshing & it makes the sales process so easy! This is exactly what I need. Your program has inspired me to finally overcome my fear and pain of selling my service to "difficult" prospects. Thanks so much for doing this and for your deep sincerity and desire to give us your very best. All of us know when we are "being sold" and when someone's heart is really in what they do and I believe yours is very much in what you do. Ari, I look forward to a long relationship with you." – *Carmen Stine*

"Profound is the only word I can think of to describe Ari's Unlock The Game program. It cuts through all the old traditional sales messages that all of us have been so conditioned to accept. Finally, someone has enough guts to stand up and say enough to the sales thinking and behaviors that have caused such negative sales stereotyping around people who aren't part of that stereotype. Ari, you have grounded me in a philosophy that is so genuine and practical that I'm already applying it to my daily selling situations." – *Alexandria Brown*

"I can't believe in all my years of selling, no one has ever had the brilliant insights to stop the chasing of prospects until now. Ari's program material is brilliant. I've never seen anyone articulate so clearly how to make the dreaded cold call into one of the most pleasant experiences in my day. I even learned how to follow–up with prospects on email by engaging them in a conversation around THEIR problems and not MY solutions. If you don't have Ari's program, you are definitely not reaching your potential." – *Tad Hargrove*

"Ari, with just one simple change in my sales process you helped me get to the truth with my prospects! I have listened to your materials several times, and here is my sense so far. I think what you have articulated and put together is profound. I have a background in psychology and several years ago I shifted out of that arena and went into selling a service I believe is fantastic. The challenge I have had, is suddenly I was being something I was not, as I tried to figure out how to dialogue with others around getting them started using my service. I have developed an internal pressure that has been gnawing at my gut for months now, and I am slowly hating the selling process. I have taken courses on how to sell, spent hours trying to figure this game out and my results are very mediocre. I kept saying to myself there has to be a way that I can be my natural self, authentic just like I was in the counseling setting. But my mindset shifted because I want to make a sale, as this is how I earn money. So I am taking on all this pressure that is getting in the way. Even though I am easy to converse with and I approach people with the idea to see if this is a fit for them or not, my deep goal is to make a sale.

When you said that the shift has to come in my own mind, that my goal is not the sale but to have a conversation instead to get to the truth, I'm thinking WOW.

I have begun to see all the ways that I have been approaching people in the context of what you are saying and I see where I am going down the wrong path and why I haven't enjoyed myself. This is going into my busiest season, and I am looking forward to changing the game I have been playing!! Thanks Ari, I am excited to continue my growth." - *Carol McWilliams*

"I'm pretty skeptical when it comes to new sales programs. Luckily I didn't let my skepticism hold me back because now I'm booking more appointments that I ever could have imagined. It really is about a different mindset, about letting go of focusing only on the sale, and saying goodbye to any fears of picking up the phone. It's so simple, yet no one in my last 20 years of selling has ever explained how to sell without pressure and by only focusing on building trust. It's amazing to make a phone call with complete ease, to be welcomed by your prospect and have them book an appointment. Selling is finally enjoyable again." – *Steve Lainer*

"Selling these days is really tough. Everyone is doing it and they are all doing it the same old traditional way. Of course we have all been trained with the old way of thinking, giving a pitch and then closing our eyes and hoping we get the application. Boy, is that painful.

Your mindset is absolutely in accordance with my personal beliefs. I hate getting sales calls myself, so now I have a mental framework to work from that makes me completely different than everyone else in the industry. I now know how to create a two–way dialogue instead of a one–way pitch. Thank you Ari, you have helped me find my personal voice." – *Eric Mercier*

"Your Mindset is right on the mark.

What you are doing is another notch above my best mentor. The way you have intertwined honesty and integrity in a business that is notoriously "salesy", is nothing short of brilliant and revolutionary. Ari, you are the new role model." – *Ben Copeland*

"Not possible. No way. I couldn't have ever imagined there was a way to sell in a humane manner, without being passive or losing my ambitions and focus. Unlock The Game has got to be the best kept secret in business today. All those books and tapes on my shelf from the "sales gurus" have gone into the trash both literally and figuratively. Ari, brilliant job. Just makes so much sense. It's always these kind of ideas that end up changing the face of business as we know it." – *Glen Sinclair*

"The mindset is really making sense to me... It's almost as if it is (or should be called) the "natural" Mindset. I have been reading and listening to a lot of other trainers and techniques and all were the traditional approaches with some change to make it appear to be different. But this is one I feel like I can stick with and will. I think the mindset applies to everything in life. Just being able to detect the pressure and knowing how to diffuse it in such a simple way. No need to escalate any conversation to a debate and a debate to a heated argument when we all should know that nothing positive comes out of that sort of exchange in the end. I know you hear this from everyone and I know everyone means every word of it. Thank you, Ari." – *James Crosswell*

"Your mindset was exactly the tool that I needed to end the chasing game with my prospects who try and disappear on me. One in particular and told me that he was seriously interested. We met, I sent him a proposal and then he was nowhere to be found. I just hate that feeling of being left hanging like that. Well, I read through your training and immediately applied what you teach about not applying pressure on the phone and using email and just like pure magic, he responded right back to me telling me the truth of where we stood. Thank you, Ari." – *Steve Ettel*

"The most important lesson I have learned is the ability to spot and give a name to the response from either the client or myself, when pressure starts building up during a sales conversation. This has given me the ability to steer the conversation very quickly away from the area where pressure is rising or adapt my approach to show more humility in order to reduce the pressure and "keep the conversation/relationship alive". I have also learned that some of my approach to sales is very similar to "unlock the game", but now instead of being this way with some of my clients (usually the ones I know the best and have the most respect for), I am actively looking at and making sure that I behave this way with all my potential and existing clients." – *Christian Pepper*

"I'm using Unlock The Game for everything I'm doing now. You are right, it's all about **TRUST** which is never discussed in any of the sales materials that I've ever come across. It's almost a no–brainer after I've gone through your program to realize there were certain behaviors I was doing that was sending my potential customers in the wrong direction. We were told to "sell, sell, sell", but no one ever gave us a "blueprint" for how to create trust in the sales process. You have, and I thank you so much for that. In the sales industry there is so much negativity and you are the only leader who has had the guts to tell us all through truth of how to make sales the most natural and authentic way. Your material is so simple, yet so powerful. Thank you for sharing with the world. We need more Ari Galpers!" – *Lynn Schreiner*

"Who says sales is challenging? With your approach, Ari, there's plenty of business out there! It only took me a few days to "get it". Ari, all I can say is that I have wasted years of quality selling time by selling the old way. I don't want to even think about all the lost opportunities I could have had if I would have found Unlock The Game earlier in my career. Ari, you rock and I can't wait to buy any future products you come out with!" – *Derrick Ruiz*

"Your program is the best kept secret around. It's funny to see all the other consulants running for the hills because they are afraid to approach potential sellers and buyers on the phone. In just a few short days after your training, I got 2 accepted offers and 3 listings worth over $750,000. Ari, everyone should be knocking at your door if they were really smart. Thank you." – *Fred Bermensolo*

" Ari, I love your Unlock The Game program. One part in particular has really made a big difference for me. It relates to a question from a seller (I'm a real estate agent) who asked why they should do business with me (my company, etc.). I said something to the effect of "Well, Mrs. Smith, I'm not necessarily sure that we should yet. May I ask you a few questions to better determine if we're a good fit?" (Or something like that). Well, Ari, she looked a little surprised at my reaction, and calmed down right away.

We both relaxed, and it got easier from that point on. I absolutely love the difference of not sounding scripted, etc. You're going to put all those old school sales trainers out of business!" – *Caroline Karolewicz*

"The fear of selling has always held me back, but not anymore. I've bought all the "salesy" programs out there, but Unlock The Game blows all that junk away. It's the most natural but effective sales approach I've ever seen. I'm now even using it in written communications with homeowners considering finding a broker to represent them in the transaction. There is no doubt that every professional should have this program. If not, they are leaving a lot of money on the table, without even knowing it. As of today, I'm throwing away all of my sales scripts taught by the "gurus" and will now rely on my own natural languaging and approach. Thank you Ari, you are a model for all of us to emulate." – *Dennis Black*

"Guess what, Ari? I've studied your training and followed your instructions to the "t"! I made all of my cold calls today. The great thing about it was all of my calls were painless. First of all, everybody seemed really happy to hear from me and they appreciated the call. Second of all and most importantly, I got over the initial hump of my cold calling fear and reluctance that was holding me back and giving me grief day in and day out. Thank you so much, Ari, can't wait to learn more!" – *Freya Childers*

 "I entered this field dreading being rejected and associated with the negative sales person stereotype. On day one in my office, I was told to play the "numbers game", be tough and don't take "no" for an answer. That was the worst advice I could have ever received. That way of thinking is exactly what feeds the negative sales person stereotype. Thank God for your program, Ari. It has revolutionized my thinking and results. My sales are up 50 percent and I feel centered and relaxed. – *Gavin Watts*

 "I have to tell you this because I'm just sitting here dumbfounded. I'd been working with a prospect for the last six months or so. Everything was going fine. The sales process was moving forward (at least I thought it was) toward a possible sale. Then, all of a sudden, she just stopped communicating with me. It was as if she had just disappeared off the face of the earth.

I did all the things I had learned from my previous sales training.

I left her messages, spoke with her assistant, sent follow-up e-mails asking about the status of the project. But nothing, not a peep.

I felt as if I had invested so much time and energy into the relationship, and she had just tossed it out the window. Right then was when I found your training. I went through it the day I got it, and put your ideas to work immediately.

I crafted an e–mail to her that applied your mindset and language, and…she responded to me 7 minutes after I sent it! I couldn't believe it! What's more, she told me the flat-out truth. She apologized for not getting back to me, said she'd been under a lot of stress on her job, and told me that the project would be on hold for another few weeks.

It felt so good to get to the truth so fast, and to know that I didn't need to get caught in the "chasing" game ever again. Thank you for showing us how we can make selling more efficient and humane."– *Diane Crawford*

 "I've been in sales for years and have read every sales book and CD I could get my hands on – I could have saved myself thousands of dollars if I would have found Unlock The Game when I started out in sales. This is the sales approach I have been looking for (and dreaming about) for years. Why do the old sales gurus have to make this process so hard? You've been able to codify the most natural and authentic approach to selling I have ever seen. We have implemented everything we have learned from you across our sales teams, in our email communication and in every way we connect with a new customer. You are the "guru" of the "gurus" that everyone should be paying attention to. Thank you, Ari, for creating Unlock The Game, it's makes sales painless and easy. – *Peter Morrissey*

"Ari, I just wanted to drop you a note and thank you for helping me put a stop to my fears of selling and helping me make my personal breakthrough that you talk about. You have created an incredible communication process that creates trust between two parties, applicable not only in sales but in every other aspect of our lives. Every day I listen to your training to remind myself that I have the skills and abilities to reach my sales goals in a way that is authentic to me. Your Mindset and languaging is how all of us feel, but no one has had the you–know–what to 'put it into a "system"'. Thank you for providing the tools necessary to help me build a natural and holistic approach to selling. Unlock The Game is life changing and I thank you for that!" – *Andy Collier*

"The moment I attended your training, I absorbed every word. It has made all of the difference in the world. I no longer have to work myself up to make a sales call and, the shift to your mindset has relaxed my style and taken a massive weight off my shoulders. I will always be a dedicated student of your teachings." – *Adam Price*

"I have been through every selling program you can imagine over the last 35 years. And I've done very well. I've made a lot of sales, but until I absorbed the Unlock The Game Mindset, I never realized how many sales I was LOSING. I picked up old selling habits that have been slowly bringing me down. What Ari has done is helped me think differently and step out of my "sales" role, so I could be myself again when I'm cold calling. What does this mean? It means I'm no longer burning opportunities with my old sales habits, I'm building trust on the phone, and I'm selling much more, and I'm happy again."–*Jerry Gasche*

"I've been looking for something like this for years. I started slowing down my dialog, lowering my voice to a relaxed natural voice, using intentional pauses and being sure to only do about 15% of the talking. Well... I connected with my prospects today and had one of the most genuine sales that I have ever had!! I was in conversation with this guy for over an hour as he told me everything that was going on in his life and we really became friends. He is joining my team and I made not only a sale but a real friend. Thank you so much, Ari, this is fantastic, I love sales again because of you and your program. Thank You, Ari, for the system that made it happen! Can't wait for tomorrow's calls!" – *Mark Galloway*

"I invested an insignificant amount of money to study the Unlock The Game mindset and up to this date, I have earned exactly $32,000 of new revenue I wouldn't have had if I hadn't learned about Ari's program. I've been in the training business for a very long time and I've seen ideas come and go. Unlock The Game is an idea ahead of its time and I just hope my competitors don't find out about it." – *Rick Itzkowich*

"My whole approach to selling has been indoctrinated over the last 11 years working for various companies. My first ever sales manager told me that 'Selling is a numbers game and you must apply pressure, pressure to get the sale.' Ari, you made me realize that way of thinking is comes from the dinosaur age of selling. Your Unlock the Game program has re-programmed my mindset completely and I now look forward to picking up the phone and having a conversation with whoever is at the other end, be it gatekeeper or decision maker. You have also taught me that approaching people from a human and humble perspective with no hidden agendas and simply talking to people and opening up a conversation about their issues, not my solutions really does work. As you state Ari, the mindset really does apply to sales people and non-sales people alike and I'm proof of that because I can now be myself which, after all, is what I'm best at." – *Chris Barnard*

"The last thing I want to be perceived as is a 'salesperson'. You have taught me a simple way of offering my services without creating the wrong impression. What's most effective is the wording and phrases you offer with Unlock The Game. What's great is that they are completely non–aggressive but at the same time effective, because they elicit the truth from the client's agenda. Now I finally have the confidence to approach someone new without compromising my professionalism and integrity. Your program has been what the accounting field has needed for years." – *Phil Hamilton*